The Walrasian Vision of the Microeconomy

The Walrasian Vision of the Microeconomy

An Elementary Exposition of
the Structure of
Modern General Equilibrium Theory

Donald W. Katzner

Ann Arbor
The University of Michigan Press

1992   1991   1990   1989   4   3   2   1

Library of Congress Cataloging-in-Publication Data

Katzner, Donald W., 1938–
  The Walrasian vision of the microeconomy: an elementary
exposition of the structure of modern general equilibrium theory /
Donald W. Katzner
      p.   cm.
  Bibliography: p.
  Includes index.
  ISBN 0-472-09409-2 (alk. paper)   — ISBN
0-472-06409-6 (pbk. : alk. paper)
    1. Microeconomics.   2. Equilibrium (Economics)   3. Walras, Leon,
1834–1910.   I. Title.
HB172.K385   1989
338.5—dc20   89-35171
                                                            CIP

Preface

To Joseph Schumpeter, " . . . the thing that comes first [in every scientific venture] is Vision. That is to say, before embarking upon analytic work of any kind we must first single out the set of phenomena we wish to investigate and acquire 'intuitively' a preliminary notion of how they hang together or, in other words, of what appear from our standpoint to be their fundamental properties. This should be obvious. If it is not, this is only owing to the fact that in practice we mostly do not start from a vision of our own but from the work of our predecessors or from ideas that float in the public mind. We then proceed to conceptualize our vision and to develop or correct it by closer examination of facts, two tasks that of necessity go together—the concepts we possess at any time and the logical relation between them suggesting further factual investigation and further factual investigation suggesting new concepts and relations. The total or 'system' of our concepts and of the relations that we establish between them is what we call a theory or a model."[1]

The vision offered on the ensuing pages is properly regarded in these terms. It is a vision of the way in which our economic world works involving the simultaneous interaction of consumers, producers, and markets. Any change occurring anywhere in the system reverberates everywhere. The vision was originally imagined by Léon Walras in his effort to explain how a particular idealized economy settles on prices for its goods.

---

1. J. A. Schumpeter, *History of Economic Analysis* (New York: Oxford University Press, 1954), 561–62.

Both for him and for much that has happened in economic science since, the need to see things as a whole has been basic. In presenting it here, the vision is described not so much by developing general characteristics, as it is by setting out a highly simplified model that springs from it. Yet particulars of the model are less important than the overall landscape that emerges. Indeed, I see the exposition of the model as the primary means of articulating the vision.

The vision itself, namely the Walrasian vision, is the same image as that conjured up in the minds of most contemporary economists as they contemplate the modern microeconomy. This vision, however, is easy to blur or miss in the process of learning microeconomic theory. There are so many things for the student to master—concepts, propositions, proofs, techniques for solving problems, topical applications, and so on—that the vision tying everything together can quickly become obscured in an avalanche of detail.

The purpose of this little volume, then, is to recreate the broad Walrasian vision as simply and as efficiently as possible for students grappling with microeconomic theory at intermediate (undergraduate) through early graduate levels. It is intended as supplementary reading to unify their thoughts. I have scrupulously tried to avoid anything that might interfere with the achievement of this aim. Consequently, many standard items have been either omitted or modified to fit the present context. To illustrate, there are no discussions of the notion of elasticity or of imperfectly competitive markets; and there are no applications, no analyses of policy options, and no exercises. Individual quantities demanded are thought of as functions of (final) output prices and prices of resources supplied by consumers, rather than of output prices and "income." And price-consumption curves, income-consumption curves, and income and substitution effects are ignored.

Moreover, the reader will find little in the way of formal argument and rigorous logic. Definitions of concepts and statements of assumptions and propositions tend, when given, to be intuitive and lack precision. There are virtually no mathematical derivations and proofs. Although mathematical symbolism is used for convenience in the transmission of certain ideas, practically all discussion is based on examples that are easily pictured geometrically in two- or three-dimensional diagrams.

These gaps of rigor and topical omission presumably will be filled in by other sources. In this regard, one possibility for more advanced students is my *Walrasian Microeconomics: An Introduction to the Economic Theory of Market Behavior* (Reading, Mass.: Addison-Wesley, 1988), from which, with a few departures, the present work was distilled. (The mathematical notation employed in these two books, however, bears little resemblance to each other.)

The prerequisites required of the reader to pursue the following pages are consistent with the aims set forth earlier. At a minimum, familiarity with an intermediate microeconomic theory text and the content of a first semester (or quarter) course in calculus is presumed. Thus it is taken for granted that the student is acquainted with such things as Edgeworth box diagrams and the derivation of consumer demand from utility maximization, and has the background to be able to use mathematical symbolism, not necessarily for derivational purposes, but as a language.

Contents

1 Introduction

On the surface, at least, modern capitalist economies seem to be chaotic. Although only "finished" products are sold, few persons actually finish the commodity toward whose production they contribute in their daily work. Fewer still consume the same goods they make. Items for personal use have to be obtained elsewhere. Furthermore, individuals, independent and overlapping groups within society, indeed societies themselves actively look out for their own interests. Cooperation is possible, but conflicts are likely and break out at all levels. Natural disasters occur. Political, social, and psychological forces impinge. And yet, somehow the thing works. There *is* order—not chaos. People, though not necessarily receiving an equitable share, generally do not starve. They have clothing, shelter, and more. Why? Subsequent pages articulate, in an elementary way, the most widely accepted contemporary vision of the way in which this comes about.

1.1 A Description of the Economy

It is appropriate to begin by describing the particular economy under consideration. The following description, which already involves considerable simplification and abstraction from reality, will serve to characterize the "actual" economic world relevant for present purposes.

A good is a material thing or service that has the capacity of directly satisfying human wants or can be used to produce something having that capacity, or both. The term commodity is synonymous with good. Final goods are passed immediately into the hands of individuals to satisfy wants. Resources are nonproduced goods needed to produce other goods. Occasionally goods produced in the past and productively used in the present, such as machinery, are referred to as resources. Intermediate goods are currently produced goods also employed in the productive process. Quantities of goods are measured in appropriate physical units.

Goods are bought and sold at prices expressed in terms of, say, dollars per unit of the good in question. Most goods are not available in unlimited quantities. Not every good, however, need be scarce. Some, such as air, may exist in sufficient quantity so as to satisfy all human wants relating to them. The prices of these goods are zero. A good has a positive price only when, relative to wants, there is not enough of it to go around.

A somewhat old-fashioned but still useful classification of resources is based on the categories of land, labor, capital, and enterprise. Land includes natural resources as well as land itself, while labor covers the variety of skilled and unskilled work the population is able to perform. The term capital refers to previously produced physical objects, like buildings and machinery, that are still employed in production. And enterprise (or entrepreneurship) is frequently defined as the willingness and ability to assume the risk of organizing and operating a business endeavor. It is a service provided by labor that is singled out for special attention. The usual names for the rewards accruing to the owners of these resources are, respectively, rents, wages, returns, and profits.

The economic activity of individuals in society takes two forms. On one hand, they provide land, labor, capital, and enterprise to firms in exchange for income. On the other, they use their income to obtain from firms the goods that satisfy their wants. In either case, although subject to certain constraints, the individual is free to choose: to work or not, which job, how to spend income, and so forth. The presence of alternatives implies that decisions must be made, and the actual alternative selected usually appears to be in the best interest of the person making the decision. Thus the individual or consumer is an important decision-making unit in the economy. Households, that is, groups of individuals acting as one unit, are treated as single individuals.

A second major type of decision-making unit is the firm. A firm is an institution that employs certain goods to produce certain other goods and also operates in its own self-interest. The goods produced are referred to as outputs; those employed in production are given the names inputs or factors. (Thus inputs, in particular, are made up of intermediate goods and resources.) As part of the process of abstraction, firms are taken to produce only a single output. Each firm must choose the method by which it transforms inputs into output. In so doing, it is both aided and confined by existing technology, that is, the pool of all knowledge concerning the methods of producing outputs from inputs. Collections of firms with similar outputs are industries.

All goods passing among individuals and/or firms, as well as payments for them, flow through markets. A market is nothing more than an institutional arrangement facilitating such exchanges. Consumers buy final goods from firms and sell resources to them in markets. Also in markets, firms buy inputs from consumers (resources) and from firms (intermediate goods), and sell their outputs (final and intermediate goods) to consumers and firms. Thus, by observing the pattern of flows through markets, it is possible to see what goods are being produced and in what quantities, with what quantities of which inputs they are being produced, how much and to which firms consumers are supplying their labor and other resources, the distribution of income across individuals, and the way final commodities are apportioned among consumers. A schematic diagram of this process is provided by figure 1-1. It should be noted that the inner flow of payments in the diagram exactly offsets the value of the outer flow of goods, that the purchase and sale of intermediate goods takes place within the box labeled "Firms," and that in moving around the circles from consumers to firms and back again, no payments or goods are lost or leak out of the system. Thus there is no banking establishment, no production for inventories, no government, and no trade with foreign countries. Of course, this picture may be expanded to include banks, inventories, government, and foreign trade, but

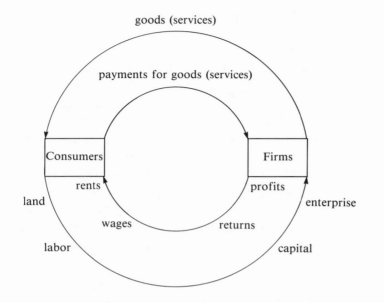

Fig. 1-1. Circular flow of goods and payments in the economy

for the time being there is much to be said for keeping matters as simple as possible.

The flows described in figure 1-1 are all flows per unit of time. This includes the flows of payments along the inner circle as well as the flows of quantities around the outer circle. In the latter case the flows of goods in the upper half of the circle are flows of outputs per unit of time. The flows of land, labor, capital, and enterprise in the lower half of the circle may be thought of as flows of productive services provided by these inputs per unit of time or, in the case of labor, as flows of the inputs themselves per unit of time.

The presence of environmental peculiarities that affect economic activity, and hence affect these flows, ought to be mentioned. For example, there are institutional rules governing property rights and commodity exchanges that emerge from a society's political and ideological background. There are also institutional requirements such as the need for decision-making units, especially firms, to record properly all economic operations in accounts expressed in terms of a standard unit of value (e.g., the dollar), and the need for all decision-making units in general to "balance" their budgets after appropriate funds have been borrowed.

Finally, the flows described above may be steady over time or they may change. Change occurs because flows of resources, and intermediate and final goods respond to price variations. Relative price increases of particular outputs tend to attract an increased flow of capital and other inputs to their production. The flow moderates with relative price declines. Firms and industries thus expand and contract.

The foregoing description of an economy has emerged from the same long tradition that engendered current economic theory itself. It is regarded here as a starting point for an analysis of general microeconomic behavior.

1.2
The Approach

Economists clarify what is going on in the economy pictured above by developing a vision of the way it operates. Their vision emphasizes the simultaneity of the decisions made by consumers and firms and the impact that any one decision has on all other decisions. It is an abstract vision, focusing only on those aspects of the economy thought to be important and ignoring that which remains. A natural method of articulating such a vision, and one frequently employed by economists, is to formulate a model.

A model of something—call the thing T—is a construct having enough in common with T so that insight into T can be obtained by studying the model. To cite a well-known example, suppose someone is asked to explain how a particular clock runs but is not permitted to remove its cover. After some observation, this person might attempt to put together gears, springs, and other parts, so as to obtain the same behavior as exhibited by the clock, and then use this model as the basis for an explanation of what makes the clock tick. In general, the model will not be an exact reproduction. Indeed, it is likely that the unseeable inner works of the clock will be different from the inner works of the model. Furthermore, the model is not unique. Many other models could be built to do the same thing. Yet, with respect to the observable behavior of the original clock, all such models and the clock are identical.

In economics, what historically has been taken to be "observable" is so-called economic data consisting of prices, quantities, incomes, and so on. Other elements such as individual preferences have been regarded as "unobservable" in the sense of being beyond the limits of the economist's knowledge. Hypotheses about these observables and unobservables and their interrelatednesses constitute the inner works of the economist's model, which is intended to reproduce the same observed behavior (data) as that generated by the unseeable inner works of the real economy. Economic models, then, do not have the physical qualities of clocks. Instead they are usually mental forms consisting of variables, parameters, assumptions, and propositions derived from them. But as in the case of the clock, they are concerned with the understanding or explanation of very specific phenomena.

In order to focus attention on the main ideas, all economic models simplify and abstract from the real world. The present model is no exception, even though the description of the economy from which it begins is already somewhat removed from reality. Further abstractions are introduced because, in formulating the model, nontrivial assumptions are made. These assumptions fall into two categories: those that shape or relate to the character of the vision that the model articulates, and those that are employed for reasons of pedagogy.

There are four major character-shaping suppositions. First, consumer tastes (preferences) and the technology available to firms are given (fixed). Second, consumers and firms simultaneously decide how much of the relevant commodities they buy and sell through an appropriate maximization procedure: consumers maximize utility (which represents preferences) subject to constraint; firms maximize profits. Third, all markets are perfectly competitive. (A market is perfectly competitive if it contains a "large" number of "small" buyers and sellers, where the number of both kinds of participants is sufficiently great and every participant is sufficiently minute so that each believes his or her actions have no influence on the market price, and therefore takes the market price as given; if the product is standardized, thus rendering inconsequential the particular seller from whom buyers make purchases; if entry is free in the sense that to become a buyer or seller is costless; and if all participants have the same complete and perfect information about all pertinent matters without uncertainty.) The fourth assumption is that within each market there are "forces" at work tending to equate demand and supply.

Models based on these four assumptions, as well as the vision of economic reality that goes with them, are usually called Walrasian, after the nineteenth-century French economist Léon Walras. Apart from the fact that the Walrasian vision is intimately intertwined with modern Western thought and culture, Walrasian models are studied because they constitute the framework within which most present-day economists think and communicate. Walrasian models, moreover, in spite of their abstractness do touch base with reality enough to have successfully shed considerable light on a variety of economic problems.[1] In addition, exploring them yields familiarity with deep and useful analytical tools having application to phenomena far beyond the boundaries of microeconomic and even economic science. And, of course, studying Walrasian models provides the means for answering the question raised at the outset: How is it possible for a vast and complex economy, motivated solely by the greed of its constituent players, to produce a coherent result and avoid general chaos?

Another important aspect of the Walrasian vision is its focus on the notion of equilibrium. Equilibrium is a situation of rest over time, a steady state: All forces "balance out" and there is no tendency for change. One common method of linking the Walrasian vision to economic reality, and the approach taken here, is to interpret what is seen at any moment in the actual economy as an equilibrium state in an appropriate Walrasian model. (An alternative perspective is to suppose that

---

1. Bits and pieces of Walrasian models have been applied to isolated observations of, and collections of empirical data gathered in, the real world. At informal levels, for example, the depiction of price movements as caused by fluctuations in demand and supply pepper newspapers and newsmagazines. More formally, consumer demand and firm production and cost functions have been estimated from actual data (e.g., A. Deaton and J. Muellbauer, *Economics and Consumer Behavior* [Cambridge University Press, 1980]; and A. A. Walters, "Production and Cost Functions: An Econometric Survey," *Econometrica* 31 [1963]: 1–66). Even full Walrasian models have been used to explain the functioning of certain specific economies such as those that arise in prisoner-of-war camps (R. A. Radford, "The Economic Organization of a P.O.W. Camp," *Economica*, n.s. 12 [1945]: 189–201).

observations, though not equilibria, are always moving toward them.) As in the case of the model of the clock described earlier, equilibrium and the ingredients (assumptions) generating it do not necessarily exist in economic reality. Rather, they constitute the inner workings of a model used to understand and explain that reality. And given the identification of observations with equilibria, to explain reality means to explain equilibrium.

As a result, the description of equilibrium or steady state becomes of paramount importance in Walrasian models. Most of what follows, therefore, is concerned with it. A "complete" dynamic model is implicit, but not spelled out. Dynamic adjustments to equilibrium from nonequilibrium positions, though occasionally mentioned, are also beyond the scope of the present volume and are largely ignored. And issues such as depreciation and the accumulation of capital and savings are not addressed.

The pedagogical assumptions employed in subsequent chapters are introduced for the sole purpose of simplifying and streamlining argument. The economic world under investigation is taken to have two outputs (final commodities), namely, a consumption good and a new capital good, each produced by a separate industry. Both goods are purchased only by consumers: the consumption good for personal consumption and the capital good as a form of saving.[2] Consumers sell labor time and rent out previously purchased (old) capital goods to firms for use in production. All units of capital, both old and new, are the same (homogeneous) as are all units of labor time, regardless of, respectively, the instant at which they are produced or the consumer from which they come. There are no other inputs and hence no intermediate goods. At each moment of decision, consumers have a given quantity of labor time to sell, and a given quantity of old capital (i.e., capital services) that has been built up from past saving to rent. They may sell less labor time than they actually have (maintaining some for leisure), but they always supply all old capital they own to firms, regardless of the amount of rent received. In spite of the homogeneity of capital, old capital manufactured in the past is a different commodity from

---

2. This is the Turgot-Smith theory of saving and investment. See J. A. Schumpeter, *History of Economic Analysis* (New York: Oxford University Press, 1954), 324.

that currently produced. Lastly, there are only two consumers in the economy and only one firm in each industry.

It should be emphasized that these pedagogical assumptions play no role other than simplification. The Walrasian vision is not blurred by exhibiting a Walrasian model that is highly specialized. A market with, say, two buyers and one seller can still be thought of as perfectly competitive as long as the participants behave as if the conditions of perfect competition obtained, for example, as if they believed that their actions had no impact on market price or, in other words, that the market dictates its price to them. Furthermore, generalization of the present model to the case of many goods, many consumers, and many firms is a straightforward expansion of the ideas developed here.[3] Even so, one still might reasonably object that the treatment of capital is less than satisfying and fraught with overlooked difficulties. For example, it is implicitly assumed that consumers earn enough to buy capital goods out of current income, that firms do not purchase them, that money capital is not required to sustain production, and so on. But once again the reader is asked to bear with this pedagogical device in order to simplify the articulation of the Walrasian vision. More cogent expositions of capital in a Walrasian model may be found elsewhere.[4]

The foregoing assumptions imply that consumers are buyers in the final commodity markets and sellers in the factor markets. Firms, on the other hand, are buyers in the factor markets and sellers in the final commodity markets. (There are no intermediate goods markets.) Thus in building the Walrasian model set forth above, it is necessary to explain the buying and selling behavior of consumers and firms as well as the interaction of these behaviors in the relevant markets. This is accomplished below by formulating models of markets, consumers, and firms in isolation before combining them to secure an overall model of the economy. Upon completion of this construction, some of the general properties of the overall model are considered.

---

3. See, for example, D. W. Katzner, *Walrasian Microeconomics: An Introduction to the Economic Theory of Market Behavior* (Reading, Mass.: Addison-Wesley, 1988).

4. E.g., *ibid.*, chaps. 12, 13.

2   Markets

The first piece of the Walrasian model to be put into place is a model of the simultaneous operation of markets. Examination of the market behavior of individual market participants is postponed to later chapters and is taken for granted here. The chapter begins descriptively by characterizing in section 2.1 the market behavior of all individuals and firms in the economy in terms of appropriate mathematical demand and supply functions. These functions are aggregated subsequently so as to encapsulate separately the demand and supply "sides" of each market. Since it is not possible to understand how markets operate together without an appreciation of the operation of a single market alone, section 2.2 first considers the workings of an isolated market in relation to equilibrium. Discussion then builds to the notion of simultaneous equilibrium in all markets at once.

2.1 Demand and Supply

The economic world under consideration encompasses four commodities, two consumers, and two firms. Each commodity is identified with a generic symbol: x for the consumption good, y for the currently produced new capital good, ℓ for labor time, and k for the old capital good produced in the past and currently rented to firms for use in production. (In this specification, all previously produced capital goods are lumped into one.) The same symbols are also used as flow variables indicating market quantities demanded, supplied, consumed, produced, or employed of the good they represent. Market prices of these goods are written as p_x, p_y, p_ℓ, p_k, respectively, where p_k actually denotes a rental value rather than a purchase price. Consumers are named 1 and 2, and firms are distinguished according to the commodity x or y they produce.

Market quantities, of course, can be broken down into smaller components. Thus the following additional variables are obtained:

x_1, x_2—amounts of x demanded or consumed by persons 1 and 2.

y_1, y_2—amounts of y demanded or consumed by persons 1 and 2.

ℓ_1, ℓ_2—amounts of ℓ supplied by persons 1 and 2.

k_1, k_2—amounts of k supplied by persons 1 and 2.

ℓ_x, ℓ_y—amounts of ℓ demanded or employed by firms producing x and y.

k_x, k_y—amounts of k (i.e., capital services) demanded or employed by firms producing x and y.

Note that when ℓ, say, represents market quantities demanded, then $\ell = \ell_x + \ell_y$. But when ℓ signifies market quantities supplied, $\ell = \ell_1 + \ell_2$.

The behavior of any participant in a market is defined as the quantities of the market good that the individual (consumer or firm) demands or supplies at various market prices. For subsequent purposes, it is convenient to describe such behavior as a response to prices in all of the markets that the individual enters, not just the particular market in question. The natural language for expressing this behavior is that of individual demand and supply functions.

Since both consumers participate in all four markets, the demand function of person 1 for good x, say, is given by

$$x_1 = D_x^1(p_x, p_y, p_\ell, p_k), \qquad (2.1\text{-}1)$$

where D_x^1 is the "name" of the function. Equation (2.1-1) means that to each possible collection of prices (i.e., values for p_x, p_y, p_ℓ, and p_k), D_x^1 assigns a unique number, x_1, which reflects the amount of good x that person 1 demands at these prices. The function indicating labor time supplied by person 2 for all sets of prices is

$$\ell_2 = S_\ell^2(p_x, p_y, p_\ell, p_k),$$

and is understood analogously to (2.1-1). Likewise, the remaining demand functions for x and y and supply functions for k and ℓ of the two individuals are

$$y_1 = D_y^1(p_x, p_y, p_\ell, p_k),$$

$$\ell_1 = S_\ell^1(p_x, p_y, p_\ell, p_k),$$

$$k_1 = S_k^1(p_x, p_y, p_\ell, p_k),$$

$$x_2 = D_x^2(p_x, p_y, p_\ell, p_k),$$

$$y_2 = D_y^2(p_x, p_y, p_\ell, p_k),$$

$$k_2 = S_k^2(p_x, p_y, p_\ell, p_k).$$

As indicated in the previous chapter, it is assumed that S_k^1 and S_k^2 are constant functions. In other words, there exist numbers $\bar{k}_1$ and $\bar{k}_2$ such that

$$\bar{k}_1 = S_k^1(p_x, p_y, p_\ell, p_k),$$
$$\bar{k}_2 = S_k^2(p_x, p_y, p_\ell, p_k), \tag{2.1-2}$$

for all p_x, p_y, p_ℓ, and p_k.

Although each firm is a buyer in both factor markets, it is a seller only in the market for its own output. Hence, the input demand functions of the firm producing x are

$$\ell_x = D_\ell^x(p_x, p_\ell, p_k),$$

$$k_x = D_k^x(p_x, p_\ell, p_k),$$

and its output supply function is

$$x = S^x(p_x, p_\ell, p_k).$$

Similarly, the demand and supply functions of the firm producing y are written as

$$\ell_y = D_\ell^y(p_y, p_\ell, p_k),$$

$$k_y = D_k^y(p_y, p_\ell, p_k),$$

$$y = S^y(p_y, p_\ell, p_k).$$

Models explaining the derivation of all of these individual demand and supply functions are presented later on. For now the functions are taken as the description of market behavior of each participant in each market.

The next step is to aggregate individual behavior into market demand and supply functions. This is done by the usual procedures of addition of functions and variables. Thus on the demand side in the market for x, addition takes place over consumers:

$$D_x(p_x, p_y, p_\ell, p_k) = D_x^1(p_x, p_y, p_\ell, p_k) + D_x^2(p_x, p_y, p_\ell, p_k),$$

$$x = x_1 + x_2,$$

so that the market demand function becomes

$$x = D_x(p_x, p_y, p_\ell, p_k).$$

Specifying p_x, p_y, p_ℓ, and p_k, then, determines individual demands x_1 and x_2 (according to individual demand functions), which are combined to obtain the market demand x at the same set of prices. Since there is only one firm participating in the market for x, the market supply function is the same as the output supply function of the firm producing x described above, or

$$x = S_x(p_x, p_\ell, p_k),$$

where

$$S_x(p_x, p_\ell, p_k) = S^x(p_x, p_\ell, p_k).$$

In this notation S_x represents the market supply function and S^x the output supply function of the firm producing x. Note also that the same symbol (x) is used to denote both market quantities demanded and market quantities supplied.

Market demand and supply functions in the market for y are obtained in the same manner as in the market for x. Hence

$$D_y(p_x, p_y, p_\ell, p_k) = D_y^1(p_x, p_y, p_\ell, p_k) + D_y^2(p_x, p_y, p_\ell, p_k),$$

$$y = y_1 + y_2,$$

and

$$y = D_y(p_x, p_y, p_\ell, p_k),$$

on the demand side, while the market supply function is

$$y = S_y(p_y, p_\ell, p_k),$$

with

$$S_y(p_y, p_\ell, p_k) = S^y(p_y, p_\ell, p_k).$$

On the demand side in the factor markets, addition takes place over firms; on the supply side, individual functions are summed across consumers. The market demand and supply functions in these two markets are given, respectively, by

$$\ell = D_\ell(p_x, p_y, p_\ell, p_k),$$

$$\ell = S_\ell(p_x, p_y, p_\ell, p_k),$$

$$k = D_k(p_x, p_y, p_\ell, p_k),$$

$$k = S_k(p_x, p_y, p_\ell, p_k),$$

where

$$D_\ell(p_x, p_y, p_\ell, p_k) = D_\ell^x(p_x, p_\ell, p_k) + D_\ell^y(p_y, p_\ell, p_k),$$

$$S_\ell(p_x, p_y, p_\ell, p_k) = S_\ell^1(p_x, p_y, p_\ell, p_k) + S_\ell^2(p_x, p_y, p_\ell, p_k),$$

$$D_k(p_x, p_y, p_\ell, p_k) = D_k^x(p_x, p_\ell, p_k) + D_k^y(p_y, p_\ell, p_k),$$

$$S_k(p_x, p_y, p_\ell, p_k) = S_k^1(p_x, p_y, p_\ell, p_k) + S_k^2(p_x, p_y, p_\ell, p_k),$$

and

$$\ell = \ell_x + \ell_y \quad \text{or} \quad \ell = \ell_1 + \ell_2,$$

$$k = k_x + k_y \quad \text{or} \quad k = k_1 + k_2.$$

Observe that D_ℓ and D_k are functions of all four price variables even though D_ℓ^x, D_ℓ^y, D_k^x, and D_k^y are functions of only three. Moreover, it follows from the supposition of equations (2.1-2) that the market supply of capital is independent of all prices:

$$\bar{k} = S_k(p_x, p_y, p_\ell, p_k),$$

where $\bar{k} = \bar{k}_1 + \bar{k}_2$. The demand and supply sides of all markets are summarized in table 2-1.

There are at least two further aspects of these demand and supply functions that should be noted. First, with all quantity variables representing flows per unit of time, one would ordinarily expect new capital produced to become a part of a larger flow of old capital in the future. That is, one would expect capital to accumulate or grow. This, in turn, might have significant impact on coming demands for both consumption and the new capital good, an eventuality that is not accounted for in the functions of table 2-1. Second, the functions of table 2-1 also exclude a market for the sale (as opposed to the rental) of old capital. Consumers wishing to draw down their stocks of previously acquired old capital would enter such a market as sellers; those desiring to increase their stocks would participate as buyers. But although these effects could be discussed within the structure of the present system, it is not worth adding the necessary complications to do so. The reason is that the primary concern here is with the description of equilibrium or steady state. And in the steady state, since there can be no change over

TABLE 2-1. Summary of the Demand and Supply Sides of Each Market

Market	Demand Side	Supply Side
Consumption good (output)	$x = D_x(p_x, p_y, p_\ell, p_k)$	$x = S_x(p_x, p_\ell, p_k)$
New capital good (output)	$y = D_y(p_x, p_y, p_\ell, p_k)$	$y = S_y(p_y, p_\ell, p_k)$
Labor time (input)	$\ell = D_\ell(p_x, p_y, p_\ell, p_k)$	$\ell = S_\ell(p_x, p_y, p_\ell, p_k)$
Old capital good (input)	$k = D_k(p_x, p_y, p_\ell, p_k)$	$\bar{k} = S_k(p_x, p_y, p_\ell, p_k)$

time, the quantity of new capital produced necessarily offsets exactly the quantity of old capital wearing out so that no growth can occur. Similarly, old capital can neither be bought nor sold in the steady state. Hence the functions of table 2-1 are quite adequate for present purposes.

It is worth pausing for a moment to point out some notational conventions employed in the symbolism introduced above. Lowercase letters denote variables, while capitals indicate functions. The letters D and S are intended to suggest, respectively, demand and supply. Subscripts on functions and price variables identify commodities. Subscripts on quantity variables and superscripts on functions refer to consumers or firms. Totals obtained by adding variables or functions across consumers or firms are signified by dropping the subscript or superscript over which the addition takes place from the appropriate symbol. Bars over price and quantity variables (such as $\bar{k}$) and the use of naughts, primes, double primes, and asterisks for superscripts (as in p_x^0, y', p_k'', and ℓ_1^*) designate specific values of the variable in question. The reader should note that these conventions will be used throughout the book.

2.2 The Operation of Markets

In Walrasian models, and indeed in the vision from which they spring, markets operate by determining price and market quantity through the interaction of demand and supply, or in other words, through the simultaneous occurrence, resolution, or balance of all market forces. The price and quantity so determined are called the (market) equilibrium price and quantity, and any observations taken in actual markets are thought of as realizations of such equilibria. Hence the model is able to explain what is seen in real-world markets.

Consider any market, say, the market for x. In formulating a model for the way the market operates, it is first necessary to specify market demand and supply functions. These are taken from section 2.1:

$$x = D_x(p_x, p_y, p_\ell, p_k),$$
$$x = S_x(p_x, p_\ell, p_k). \tag{2.2-1}$$

Economists often picture demand and supply functions geometrically in terms of two-dimensional diagrams that relate the quantity of a good per unit of time to its price. This can be done only if the prices of all other goods (in the present case, p_y, p_ℓ, and p_k) are held fixed. Thus, for example, set $p_y = p'_y$, $p_\ell = p'_\ell$, and $p_k = p'_k$. Then the functions D_x and S_x of (2.2-1) each reduce to a function of the single variable p_x:

$$x = D_x(p_x, p'_y, p'_\ell, p'_k),$$

$$x = S_x(p_x, p'_\ell, p'_k).$$

(2.2-2)

Such functions are usually drawn as the demand and supply curves appropriately labeled in figure 2-l(a). Note that common practice in economics places the dependent variable (x) on the horizontal axis, and the independent variable (p_x) on the vertical. Thus the graphs actually appearing in the diagram and labeled as D_x and S_x would not ordinarily be interpreted as those of D_x and S_x but, rather, as those of their inverses. Because the diagram is intended only to illustrate a simple case in which inverses normally exist and look something like the curves really intended, problems do not arise by adhering to this tradition. But the reversal of mathematical convention should be kept in mind.

In general, equilibrium is a situation in which there is no tendency to change. With respect to equations (2.2-2) and figure 2-l(a), then, any point (x, p_x) is an equilibrium if at that point no consumer or firm is attempting to alter his or its market behavior. Hence for the simultaneous occurrence of the equations of (2.2-2) to describe equilibrium in the model (given the fixed values for p_y, p_ℓ, and p_k), it must be established as a logical proposition that intersection points such as (x^0, p_x^0) in figure 2-l(a) and only those points have this equilibrium property. As long as prices and quantities are restricted to be positive, the argument is trivial: at (x^0, p_x^0) in figure 2-l(a), firms and consumers buy and sell what they wish. There is no need to vary behavior. Conversely, at any other price in the diagram, either firms cannot sell all they produce or consumers cannot buy all they want. In other words, at any quantity different from x^0, either firms could not receive the price they require for their

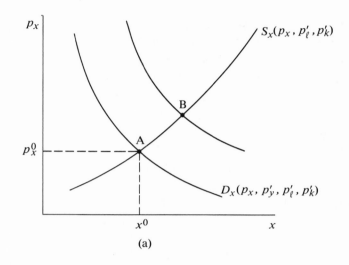

(a)

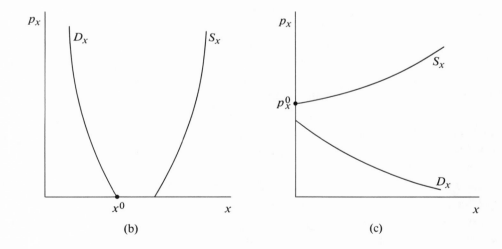

(b) (c)

Fig. 2-1. Equilibrium in an isolated market

output, or consumers would have to pay more than they wish. In either case the result is a change in behavior as consumers and firms successfully compete to modify price and quantity in an effort to reach their goals. With these (hypothetical) movements going on, equilibrium cannot prevail. Thus, for positive prices and quantities, there is a logical identification between equilibria and intersection points. But once the possibility of a zero price or quantity is admitted, the proposition breaks down. Figure 2-l(b) shows a market equilibrium at $(x^0, 0)$ with supply unequal to demand.   Any forces in the market pushing price towards negative values are exactly offset by the floor of zero below which prices are not permitted to fall. Similarly $(0, p_x^0)$ is an equilibrium in figure 2-l(c) but not an intersection point of the demand and supply curves. A parallel argument applies to each set of values p_y', p_ℓ', and p_k'.

The critical role the notion of equilibrium plays in the present depiction of the Walrasian vision should be emphasized. Suppose an investigator were to observe the actual market at a given moment in time. All that could be seen is that at some price, say p_x^0, so many units of the commodity, say x^0, were sold. The investigator's observation would consist of the market flow represented by the single point A in a diagram such as figure 2-l(a). There would be no empirical evidence to suggest the existence in reality of either the demand function D_x or supply function S_x . How is this observation to be understood? What sense can be made of it? One plausible interpretation is to assume that unseeable demand and supply curves exist and that they happen to intersect at A. Thus a model explaining the observed flow as a market equilibrium position is obtained in much the same way as the model of the clock explains the clock's behavior (sec. 1.2). Furthermore, if a subsequent observation produced, say, the point B in figure 2-l(a), and if there were reason to believe that the original supply curve had remained unchanged and went through B, then the investigator has a ready explanation for the change: there was an increase in demand that shifted the equilibrium from A to B.

On this view, the concept of equilibrium provides the crucial link between the model and reality. No empirical tests are required. It is a matter of interpretation. Moreover, the question of whether a unique equilibrium exists is vital. If demand and supply curves did not intersect, and if equilibrium did not occur at a zero quantity or price (e.g., interchange the labels of the demand and supply curves in figure 2-1(b)), then the model could have no relevance for the real world. Since equilibrium would not exist in the model, it would be impossible to identify equilibrium with any observed point. The uniqueness problem is also significant. If demand and supply curves intersected more than once, then the model would be incomplete. It would admit the possibility of many equilibria as theoretical descriptions of reality without indicating the appropriate one to employ. Lastly, the model must exhibit a certain kind of stability. For if equilibria were unstable, then the change in the model that produced the shift in demand, and hence movement away from A, could not result in convergence toward B. Hence the model could not explain the observed passage from A to B.

It is possible to be more explicit about the market effects of the hypothetical behavior of consumers and firms when the market is out of equilibrium. Thus one might postulate that if quantity demanded were to exceed quantity supplied at any price, then the ensuing competition would force that price to rise. Similarly, were quantity demanded to fall short of quantity supplied, price would tend to fall. However, the formal examination of such market "laws of motion" in terms of mathematical difference or differential equations is beyond the scope of the present study. Suffice it to say instead that since the approach taken here always links observations of reality with equilibria in the model, the dynamic working out of equilibrium from a nonequilibrium position, like the demand and supply curves themselves, cannot be seen in the actual economic world.

Observe from equations (2.2-2) that the increase in demand required to move from A to B in figure 2-1(a) can come about only with a change in one or more of the prices of the other goods, namely p'_y, p'_ℓ, and p'_k. (Since the supply curve has been assumed fixed in figure 2-1(a), it may be supposed that the change has occurred in p'_y alone.) Now all demand and supply curves (except S_y) in the remaining markets, if they had been drawn as in figure 2-1(a) with the market for x taken to be in equilibrium at point A, would have originally been drafted for $p_x = p_x^0$. But when p_x^0 rises as a result of the increase in demand for x, these curves also move, causing further variations in p_y, p_ℓ, and p_k, and hence further changes in the market for x. Markets, therefore, are interrelated: modification in any one reverberates throughout all others. When all such interacting modulations have ceased, the four markets of table 2-1 can be in equilibrium together. This simultaneous equilibrium or steady state is described by:

$$D_x(p_x, p_y, p_\ell, p_k) = S_x(p_x, p_\ell, p_k),$$

$$D_y(p_x, p_y, p_\ell, p_k) = S_y(p_y, p_\ell, p_k),$$

$$\quad (2.2\text{-}3)$$

$$D_\ell(p_x, p_y, p_\ell, p_k) = S_\ell(p_x, p_y, p_\ell, p_k),$$

$$D_k(p_x, p_y, p_\ell, p_k) = \bar{k}.$$

Values for market equilibrium prices are obtained as the simultaneous solution[1] of (2.2-3); values for market equilibrium quantities are found by substitution of these market-equilibrium-price values into the demand or supply equations of table 2-1. (Values for individual quantities at this equilibrium may be secured by substituting the same price values into the appropriate individual demand and supply equations of sec. 2.1.) The dynamic process of adjustment as all market-interacting changes resolve themselves is not pursued.

It should be pointed out that, although lacking explicit description, there is an implicit interest rate variable in this model. That is, once p_y and p_k are determined, a value for an interest rate linking the prices of old and new capital goods can always be found. In other articulations of the Walrasian vision, the value of such an inter temporal variable might independently emerge from, say, the interaction of demand and supply in a bond market. But regardless, the rate of interest is of little importance in the particular model developed here.

Finally, the reader should be aware that three of the assumptions imposed on markets to ensure perfect competition (sec. 1.2) also are implicit in preceding discussion. The requirement

---

1. Actually, it turns out that there are not enough independent equations in (2.2-3) to obtain unique values for all equilibrium prices. See section 6.2.

that all market participants take prices as parameters which they believe they cannot influence permits individual quantities demanded and supplied to be expressed as functions of prices. If individual consumers and firms could control market prices and behaved accordingly, then prices could not appear as independent variables in their demand and supply functions. The stipulation that products within markets be standardized allows the adding up of individual demand and supply functions and quantities to obtain market demand and supply functions and quantities. And the restriction that all market participants have identical information on all relevant matters ensures that all buyers and sellers within a given market exchange goods at the same price. The free-entry property does not become significant until the long-run behavior of the firm is considered in chapter 5.

3   Individual Consumer Behavior

According to section 2.1, the economic behavior of consumers participating in markets is completely described by their individual demand and supply functions. In the notation of that section, the demand and supply functions for person 1 are

$$x_1 = D_x^1(p_x, p_y, p_\ell, p_k),$$

$$y_1 = D_y^1(p_x, p_y, p_\ell, p_k),$$

$$\ell_1 = S_\ell^1(p_x, p_y, p_\ell, p_k),$$

$$k_1 = S_k^1(p_x, p_y, p_\ell, p_k),$$

while those for person 2 are

$$x_2 = D_x^2(p_x, p_y, p_\ell, p_k),$$

$$y_2 = D_y^2(p_x, p_y, p_\ell, p_k),$$

$$\ell_2 = S_\ell^2(p_x, p_y, p_\ell, p_k),$$

$$k_2 = S_k^2(p_x, p_y, p_\ell, p_k).$$

The intent of the next several paragraphs is to present another piece of the Walrasian model under consideration here, which is properly regarded as a model in its own right, and which explains how these functions arise. As indicated in section 1.2, this explanation (since it is Walrasian in character) is based on the assumptions that (i) the preferences of consumers are fixed,

(ii) the buying and selling decisions consumers make are the outcome of constrained utility (preference) maximization, and (iii) in making decisions consumers take prices as parameters over which they have no control (perfect competition). Of course, none of these assumptions can be directly verified since only the behavior of consumers, that is, the outcome of their decision-making activity, can be observed. Because it is assumed for pedagogical purposes (sec. 1.2) that the quantities of old capital supplied (k_1 and k_2) are set and do not vary in response to market price changes, there is nothing about the capital supply functions (S_k^1 and S_k^2) that requires elucidation. In what follows, then, these functions are ignored.

Section 3.1 introduces the concept of utility function as a representation of individual preferences. Indifference surfaces that arise from utility functions are described next, and then the properties of each are discussed. Budget constraints and utility maximization subject to the budget constraint are the topics of section 3.2. The definition of consumer demand and supply functions as the outcome of constrained utility maximization is taken up in section 3.3, as are the properties these functions must possess by dint of their derivation from utility maximization.

It should be noted that, unlike the model of firm behavior developed in chapters 4 and 5, no distinction is made here between the "long run" and the "short run."[1] The same explanation of consumer demand and supply functions applies to either case.

3.1 Utility Functions

The things among which a consumer has preferences are baskets of commodities. The baskets relevant for present purposes contain various quantities of the consumption good x, the new capital good y, and an additional commodity called leisure time and denoted by z. (Leisure time is included so as to be able to gain a handle on labor supply.) Although no limits are placed on the quantities of x and y that might appear in baskets, the individual is typically assumed to have only a finite amount of available time, α. For example, if the time available is taken to

---

1. Meanings for the terms *long run* and *short run* are given in section 4.1.

be a single day, and if time is measured in units of hours, then $\alpha = 24$. Time, moreover, may be used either as leisure time (z) or as labor time (ℓ). (Entrepreneurship is supplied during the time that the consumer works.) Hence, a basket for person 1 containing z_1 units of leisure time implies a labor time for that individual of $\ell_1 = \alpha - z_1$. A similar equation obtains for person 2, namely $\ell_2 = \alpha - z_2$, where α is the same for each person. Furthermore, a basket for person 1, say, with y_1 units of the new capital good, is a basket in which this individual is saving $y_1 p_y$ out of current income, where p_y is determined by the market as described in section 2.2.

For the moment, continue to focus attention on person 1. This person's baskets of commodities are written (x_1, y_1, z_1) and the collection of all such baskets he (or she) may consider, that is, his commodity space, is

$$\{(x_1, y_1, z_1): x_1 \geq 0, \ y_1 \geq 0, \ \text{and} \ \alpha \geq z_1 \geq 0\}.$$

Assume person 1 is either indifferent between all pairs of baskets in his commodity space or, for those pairs of baskets between which he is not indifferent, always prefers one basket to the other. Assume further that these preferences and indifferences are represented in (utility) numbers, μ_1, assigned to each basket and having the property that within any given pair, the more preferred basket has the higher number. If the baskets are indifferent, then the same number is given to each. Taking all numerical assignments together describes a utility function for person 1,

$$\mu_1 = U^1(x_1, y_1, z_1),$$

defined on his commodity space, where U^1 is the symbolic name of the function. It is clear that for any pair of baskets (x_1', y_1', z_1') and (x_1'', y_1'', z_1'') that are in the commodity space, $U(x_1', y_1', z_1') > U(x_1'', y_1'', z_1'')$ if and only if (x_1', y_1', z_1') is preferred to (x_1'', y_1'', z_1''), and $U(x_1', y_1', z_1') = U(x_1'', y_1'', z_1'')$ whenever (x_1', y_1', z_1') and (x_1'', y_1'', z_1'') are indifferent. The only significance of utility numbers is that they reflect ordering of baskets by preference. Beyond this the numbers have no meaning. Thus, for example, the utility function

$$U^1(x_1, y_1, z_1) = x_1 y_1 z_1$$

contains exactly the same information as

$$U^1(x_1, y_1, z_1) = (x_1 y_1 z_1)^2.$$

Such utility functions are often referred to as ordinal utility functions.

Note that by treating the new capital good y, which is also interpreted as saving, as a component of the baskets among which the consumer has the preferences and indifferences described above, the motivation for individual saving accommodated by this model is highly simplistic. (This limitation is in addition to those already described in sec. 1.2.) Here the individual saves only for the pleasure of saving, ignoring whatever risks and possibilities for future consumption that actual saving implies. Moreover, since y_1 is required to be nonnegative, person 1 is not permitted to dissave, that is, to "borrow" new capital and enter the market for y as a seller rather than as a buyer. The possibility that he might dissave by selling some of his previously acquired (old) capital already has been precluded by confining discussion to the steady state in which no such sales can occur.

Let (x_1^0, y_1^0, z_1^0) be a basket in the commodity space of person 1. The indifference surface through (x_1^0, y_1^0, z_1^0) is the set of all baskets, including (x_1^0, y_1^0, z_1^0), which are indifferent to (x_1^0, y_1^0, z_1^0), or

$$\{(x_1, y_1, z_1): U^1(x_1, y_1, z_1) = U^1(x_1^0, y_1^0, z_1^0)\}.$$

With $\mu_1^0 = U^1(x_1^0, y_1^0, z_1^0)$, the equation of the indifference surface through (x_1^0, y_1^0, z_1^0) (or now the μ^0 indifference surface), is frequently obtained by solving $\mu_1^0 = U^1(x_1, y_1, z_1)$ for, say, y_1 as a function of x_1 and z_1. To illustrate, if the utility function were $U^1(x_1, y_1, z_1) = x_1 y_1 z_1$, then the equation of the μ^0 indifference surface, for any $\mu^0 > 0$, would be given by

$$y_1 = \frac{\mu_1^0}{x_1 z_1}.$$

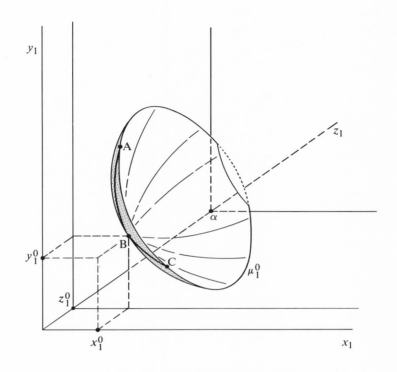

Fig. 3-1. Indifference bowl through (x_1^0, y_1^0, z_1^0)

There is one indifference surface through each basket in the commodity space. The collection of all indifference surfaces is called the indifference map.

With a three-dimensional commodity space, indifference surfaces often have the shape of bowls, as the one through (x_1^0, y_1^0, z_1^0) pictured in figure 3-1. (Observe in this diagram that, since z_1 cannot exceed α, the commodity space is cut off by the plane perpendicular to the z_1 axis at α. Furthermore, although a bowl of only finite size is drawn, the actual indifference surface extends infinitely far out from the origin or until it intersects the boundary of the commodity space.) By holding one variable, say z_1, fixed, two-dimensional sections of both the commodity space and indifference surface are obtained. For example, setting $z_1 = z_1^0$ in figure 3-1 limits attention to those baskets of the commodity space in the plane perpendicular to the z_1 axis at z_1^0. The indifference surface restricted to that plane reduces to the curve labeled ABC. All baskets on both the curve and surface have the same utility value, namely, $\mu_1^0 = U^1(x_1^0, y_1^0, z_1^0)$. Each shift in the value of z_1^0 results in a new μ_1^0 indifference curve (i.e., a new section of the μ_1^0 indifference surface) in a different plane. Requiring y_1 (or x_1) to be fixed instead of z_1 would lead to similar conclusions with the roles of z_1 and y_1 (or z_1 and x_1) interchanged.

In addition to the fact that every basket of commodities lies on a single indifference surface, it is also true that many baskets have three "marginal utilities" associated with them. Marginal utilities are important because they provide a simple and appealing means for characterizing those baskets that maximize utility as described in the next section. Given a particular ordinal utility function, there are two ways to introduce the notion of marginal utility. In both cases a calculation of marginal utility is potentially possible with respect to each good at each basket in the commodity space having all of its components positive. (The set of all such baskets constitutes the interior of the commodity space.) The marginal utility of person 1 with respect to x at (x_1^0, y_1^0, z_1^0) is either expressed in approximate form as a ratio of finite increments, that is,

$$MU_x^1(x_1^0, y_1^0, z_1^0) = \frac{U^1(x_1^0 + \Delta x_1, y_1^0, z_1^0) - U^1(x_1^0, y_1^0, z_1^0)}{\Delta x_1},$$

where Δx_1 is a "small" number, or in exact form as the (partial) derivative

$$MU_x^1(x_1^0, y_1^0, z_1^0) = \lim_{\Delta x_1 \to 0} \frac{U^1(x_1^0 + \Delta x_1, y_1^0, z_1^0) - U^1(x_1^0, y_1^0, z_1^0)}{\Delta x_1}.$$

No distinction is made between these two forms in subsequent discussion. If the reader wishes to think in terms of the approximate form, however, appropriate equal signs should properly be interpreted as approximate equalities. Note that employing the approximate form with $\Delta x_1 = 1$, $MU_x^1(x_1^0, y_1^0, z_1^0)$ becomes the additional utility obtained by person 1 upon adding one more unit of x to the basket (x_1^0, y_1^0, z_1^0). The marginal utilities of person 1 with respect to y_1 and z_1 at (x_1^0, y_1^0, z_1^0) are defined analogously and are denoted, respectively, by $MU_y^1(x_1^0, y_1^0, z_1^0)$ and $MU_z^1(x_1^0, y_1^0, z_1^0)$.

Now consider a basket (x_1^0, y_1^0, z_1^0) in the interior of person 1's commodity space. Think of z_1 as being held fixed at z_1^0 so that a picture of the μ^0 indifference curve resembling curve ABC in figure 3-1 is secured. Then it turns out that the slope of this indifference curve at (x_1^0, y_1^0, z_1^0) may be computed as the negative of a ratio of marginal utilities:

$$-\frac{MU_x^1(x_1^0, y_1^0, z_1^0)}{MU_y^1(x_1^0, y_1^0, z_1^0)}.$$

If y_1 were held fixed at y_1^0 instead of z_1 at z_1^0, then the slope of the corresponding indifference curve through (x_1^0, y_1^0, z_1^0) would, at the same basket, be

$$-\frac{MU_x^1(x_1^0, y_1^0, z_1^0)}{MU_z^1(x_1^0, y_1^0, z_1^0)}.$$

These ratios without the minus signs are usually called the marginal rates of substitution of x for y at (x_1^0, y_1^0, z_1^0) and, respectively, of x for z at (x_1^0, y_1^0, z_1^0) as person 1 moves along the appropriate indifference curve. They evidently reflect the rates at which person 1 may substitute one commodity for another while maintaining a constant level of utility. The marginal rate of substitution of y for z and the slope of the associated indifference curve are obtained similarly. Although each marginal utility function by itself depends on the particular ordinal utility function in use, the marginal rates of substitution do not.

In addition to assuming that preferences and indifferences, and a utility function representing them, exist for person 1, it is also necessary to impose sufficient restrictions on the utility function so that appropriate constrained utility maximization (to be discussed in the next section) can be carried out. (Recall that the notions of fixed consumer tastes and maximization are cornerstones of the Walrasian vision.) One collection of assumptions that does the job nicely is as follows: Suppose (i) that the utility function is continuous throughout the commodity space and that all marginal utilities can be calculated (continuously, when expressed in derivative form) at every interior basket; (ii) that a larger basket of commodities (one containing more of at least one commodity and no less of all others) is always preferred to a smaller basket; (iii) that all indifference surfaces in the interior of the commodity space are strictly convex (i.e., the straight line segment connecting any two distinct baskets on any such indifference surface lies, except for its end points, entirely above the surface); and (iv) that if an indifference surface contains at least one basket in the interior of the commodity space, then all baskets of the indifference surface also lie in the interior of the commodity space. Assumption (ii) implies that all marginal utilities are positive at every interior basket and hence, since their slopes are the negatives of ratios of marginal utilities, that all interior indifference curves, such as curve ABC in figure 3-1, are everywhere downward sloping. Assumption (iii) means that along, say, the same indifference curve, the marginal rate of substitution diminishes as x_1 rises: for the less person 1 has of y when taking one more unit of it away, the more he has to be compensated with the other good in order to remain on that curve. And assumption (iv) says that no indifference surface in the interior of the commodity space can run into the x_1-y_1, x_1-z_1, or y_1-z_1 planes that make up part of the boundary of the commodity space.

Finally, it should be remarked that the above discussion, including concepts, notation and assumptions, applies in exactly the same detail for person 2, with the number 2 replacing the number 1 in the relevant places. Thus, for example, person 2's utility function is written as

$$\mu_2 = U^2(x_2, y_2, z_2),$$

his marginal utilities at (x_2^0, y_2^0, z_2^0) are $MU_x^2(x_2^0, y_2^0, z_2^0)$, $MU_y^2(x_2^0, y_2^0, z_2^0)$, and $MU_z^2(x_2^0, y_2^0, z_2^0)$, and the assumptions imposed on his preferences, indifferences, and utility function are identical to those prescribed for person 1.

3.2 Utility Maximization

The environment in which the consumer makes buying and selling decisions is set by the economy's markets as they determine values for prices p_x, p_y, p_ℓ, and p_k. Once a collection of price values is given, the expenditure on final commodities required to obtain any basket of commodities can be found along with the income from the sale of the labor time that this same basket implies. In addition, the consumer receives income from the rental of previously purchased (old) capital and from firm profits as the reward for entrepreneurship. (Recall fig. 1-1 and remember that the factor of land has been dropped from consideration.)

To be specific, return to the case of person 1. The expenditure necessary to secure basket (x_1, y_1, z_1) is

$$x_1 p_x + y_1 p_y,$$

where $x_1 p_x$ represents "consumption" expenditure and $y_1 p_y$ is interpreted as "expenditure" on saving. The income this basket generates is $\ell_1 p_\ell$, where

$$\ell_1 = \alpha - z_1, \tag{3.2-1}$$

and α is total time available. Further income consists of $\bar{k}_1 p_k$, where $\bar{k}_1$ denotes the fixed quantity of old capital rented to firms by person 1, and $\beta_1(\pi_x + \pi_y)$, where π_x and π_y are the respective profits[2] of the firm producing x and the firm producing y, and β_1 is the fraction of $\pi_x + \pi_y$ accruing to person 1. In the present context, β_1 is taken as a fixed number already set by the past activity of the individual. With values of p_x, p_y, p_ℓ, and p_k given, π_x and π_y are also determined.[3] Person 1's total income,

---

2. Actually, π_x and π_y turn out to be the maximum profit that the firms are able to achieve, given market prices. See chapter 5.

3. For the firm producing x, substitute given price values along with the profit-maximizing values of x, ℓ_x, and k_x into (5.1-2) to obtain π_x. Similar substitutions into an analogous equation yield π_y.

m_1, associated with the basket (x_1, y_1, z_1) is therefore

$$m_1 = \ell_1 p_\ell + \bar{k}_1 p_k + \beta_1(\pi_x + \pi_y). \qquad (3.2\text{-}2)$$

The fixity of $\bar{k}_1$ and β_1 deserve comment. In general, recall, $\bar{k}_1$ may actually grow over time as new capital is produced and added to existing stock. But in the steady state, $\bar{k}_1$ remains constant because the new capital purchased by person 1 exactly offsets the old capital in his (or her) possession that has worn out. Since attention here is focused on the steady state, one may reasonably suppose that $\bar{k}_1$ is constant. Turning to β_1, note that although all labor is homogeneous, it is used in different ways by the firm. That portion of it providing entrepreneurial services has a reward in the form of firm profit returned to its provider. This latter reward is in addition to p_ℓ, which only pays the individual for labor time (per unit of labor time) spent in the firm regardless of the specific activities performed while there. The entrepreneurial activity engaged in by each employee is assumed to be an institutional constant determined by the firms—hence, so is β_1. Observe also that in any particular case, the entrepreneurial services supplied by person 1 are likely to be different for firm x than for firm y. Indeed, person 1 may only work for one of the two firms. Thus there really should be a separate β_1 for each firm. However, for purposes of simplification, it is convenient and harmless to suppose, as is implied above, that β_1 is the same for both.

Assume that in making purchase and sales decisions, the consumer is not permitted to spend more than income received. Then person 1 is limited to baskets in his commodity space that satisfy the inequality

$$x_1 p_x + y_1 p_y \leq \ell_1 p_\ell + \bar{k}_1 p_k + \beta_1(\pi_x + \pi_y),$$

or, upon substitution of (3.2-1),

$$x_1 p_x + y_1 p_y + z_1 p_\ell \leq \alpha p_\ell + \bar{k}_1 p_k + \beta_1(\pi_x + \pi_y).$$

The collection of all such baskets is called person 1's budget set. The boundary of the budget set that runs through the interior of the commodity space is the budget plane. And the equation of the budget plane, namely,

$$x_1 p_x + y_1 p_y + z_1 p_\ell = \alpha p_\ell + \bar{k}_1 p_k + \beta_1(\pi_x + \pi_y), \qquad (3.2\text{-}3)$$

is the budget constraint.

Notice that what has been called person 1's expenditure, namely $x_1 p_x + y_1 p_y$, is part of the schematic flow along the upper section of the inner circle in figure 1-1. Likewise, the income of person 1, as described by (3.2-2), is part of the flow along the lower section of the same circle. The budget constraint (3.2-3) asserts that this expenditure is the same as this income. Hence, combining (3.2-3) with a similar constraint for person 2 (see sec. 6.1 and app. 6.A in chap. 6) implies that the aggregate flow along the upper section equals the aggregate flow along the lower section. Nothing can be lost, then, as payments flow around the inner circle of figure 1-1.

An illustration of a budget plane for person 1 appears as the shaded triangle in figure 3-2 for the special case in which $\bar{k}_1 p_k + \beta_1(\pi_x + \pi_y) = 0$ and hence in which $m_1 = \ell_1 p_\ell$, where ℓ_1 varies with z_1 according to (3.2-1). The x intercept of the plane is m_1/p_x, the y intercept is m_1/p_y ($z_1 = 0$ for both the x and y intercepts so that $m_1 = \alpha p_\ell$), and the z intercept is α. Clearly, if person 1 does not work, then he cannot afford to buy either x or y. The baskets enclosed by the three coordinate planes and positioned on and beneath the budget plane constitute the budget set. As with indifference surfaces, the budget plane appears as a two-dimensional budget line when one of x_1, y_1, or z_1 is fixed at a specific value. For example, setting $z_1 = z_1^0$ with market prices given and $\bar{k}_1 p_k + \beta_1(\pi_x + \pi_y) = 0$, and combining equations (3.2-1)–(3.2-3), the budget constraint shrinks to

$$x_1 p_x + y_1 p_y = m_1^0, \qquad (3.2\text{-}4)$$

where $m_1^0 = (\alpha - z_1^0)p_\ell$. The graph of (3.2-4) lies in the plane perpendicular to the z_1 axis at z_1^0, and is shown as the line DE

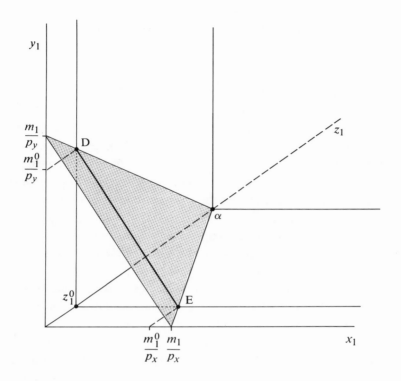

Fig. 3-2. Budget plane: $\bar{k}_1 p_k + \beta_1(\pi_x + \pi_y) = 0$

in figure 3-2. Its slope is

$$-\frac{p_x}{p_y}.$$

A similar budget line with slope

$$-\frac{p_x}{p_\ell}$$

would obtain if y_1 were fixed and z_1 played the role of y_1 in the above.

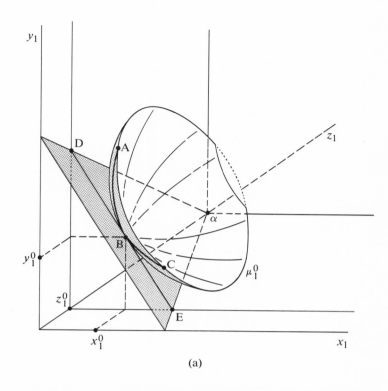

(a)

Fig. 3-3(a). Utility maximization subject to the budget constraint

The last assumption to be imposed in the present development of an explanation of consumer demand and supply functions is that, in making decisions, the individual always buys commodities and sells factors so as to maximize utility over an appropriate budget set. In other words, the most preferred basket is always chosen out of those available. To illustrate, let prices be dictated by the markets and suppose, given these prices, that the (constrained) utility-maximizing basket for person 1 is (x_1^0, y_1^0, z_1^0). Then at (x_1^0, y_1^0, z_1^0), an indifference surface is tangent to a budget plane in the commodity space. This is shown in figure 3-3(a), which is actually a combination of figures 3-1 and 3-2. In the plane perpendicular to the z_1 axis at z_1^0, the same tangency materializes as a tangency between indifference curve ABC and budget line DE as indicated both by figure 3-3(a) and separately by figure 3-3(b). An example of a tangency involving

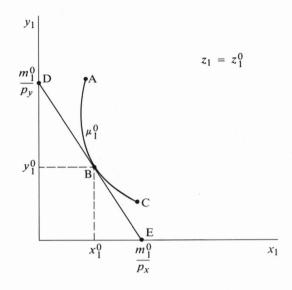

Fig. 3-3(b). Utility maximization subject to the budget constraint

a budget plane with $\bar{k}_1 p_k + \beta_1(\pi_x + \pi_y) > 0$, that is, for which person 1 has positive nonwage income, is drawn in figure 3-3(c). Enough has been assumed about the utility function to ensure that in all cases a unique utility-maximizing basket always exists for any collection of positive prices specified by the market, that the utility-maximizing basket always lies on the budget plane (from assumption (ii) of sec. 3.1), and that it cannot lie on any of the three coordinate planes that bound the commodity space (from assumption (iv) of sec. 3.1).

From the geometry of figures 3-3(a) and 3-3(b), the slope, at (x_1^0, y_1^0, z_1^0), of the indifference curve in the plane perpendicular to the z_1 axis at z_1^0, is the same as that of the budget line or, dropping minus signs,

$$\frac{p_x}{p_y} = \frac{MU_x^1(x_1^0, y_1^0, z_1^0)}{MU_y^1(x_1^0, y_1^0, z_1^0)}. \tag{3.2-5}$$

Analogously, with y_1 fixed at y_1^0 in place of z_1 set at z_1^0, it may

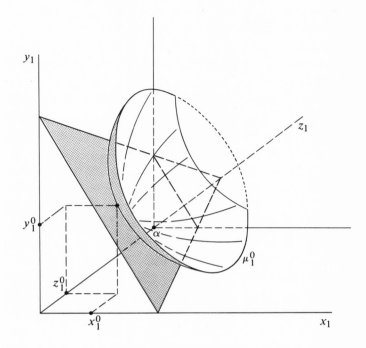

Fig. 3-3(c). Utility maximization subject to the budget constraint

be concluded, also at the maximum, that

$$\frac{p_x}{p_\ell} = \frac{MU_x^1(x_1^0, y_1^0, z_1^0)}{MU_z^1(x_1^0, y_1^0, z_1^0)}. \qquad (3.2\text{-}6)$$

Thus marginal rates of substitution must equal price ratios if utility is to be maximized subject to the budget constraint. Combining (3.2-5) and (3.2-6) yields

$$\begin{aligned}
\frac{MU_x^1(x_1^0, y_1^0, z_1^0)}{p_x} &= \frac{MU_y^1(x_1^0, y_1^0, z_1^0)}{p_y}, \\
&= \frac{MU_z^1(x_1^0, y_1^0, z_1^0)}{p_\ell}, \qquad (3.2\text{-}7)
\end{aligned}$$

which asserts, using the approximate concept of marginal utility, that the marginal utilities per dollar provided by purchasing the last increment of each good equalize at the maximum.[4]

Equations (3.2-5) and (3.2-6) are first-order conditions for the maximization of the utility function subject to the budget constraint. They can easily be derived using the calculus. That these first-order conditions actually identify maximizing (as opposed to, say, minimizing) baskets is guaranteed by the suppositions that a larger basket of commodities is always preferred to a smaller one (assumption (ii) in sec. 3.1) and that all interior indifference surfaces are strictly convex (assumption (iii) in sec. 3.1).

3.3 Consumer Demand and Supply Functions

Under the assumptions of sections 3.1 and 3.2, the consumer demand and supply functions listed at the beginning of this chapter (excluding S_k^1 and S_k^2) can be explained as the outcome of constrained utility maximization by persons 1 and 2 as prices hypothetically vary over all positive real numbers. To do so requires that, even though the decision-making process of the individual cannot be seen, statements of the form, "the values p_x', p_y', p_ℓ', p_k', x_1', y_1', and $\ell_1' = \alpha - z_1'$ satisfy the equations

$$x_1 = D_x^1(p_x, p_y, p_\ell, p_k),$$

$$y_1 = D_y^1(p_x, p_y, p_\ell, p_k), \qquad (3.3\text{-}1)$$

$$\ell_1 = S_\ell^1(p_x, p_y, p_\ell, p_k),"$$

be interpreted to mean that "(x_1', y_1', z_1') maximizes $U^1(x_1, y_1, z_1)$ subject to

$$x_1 p_x' + y_1 p_y' + z_1 p_\ell' \leq \alpha p_\ell' + \bar{k}_1 p_k' + \beta_1(\pi_x' + \pi_y'), " \qquad (3.3\text{-}2)$$

where π_x' and π_y' are determined from p_x', p_y', p_ℓ', and p_k' as described in note 3 for this chapter (see p. 33). Since unique utility-maximizing baskets of commodities exist and are

---

4. In view of the fact that the system developed here is unable to determine unique values for p_x, p_y, and p_ℓ (sec. 6.2), the ratios of (3.2-7) only have meaning relative to a suitable price normalization.

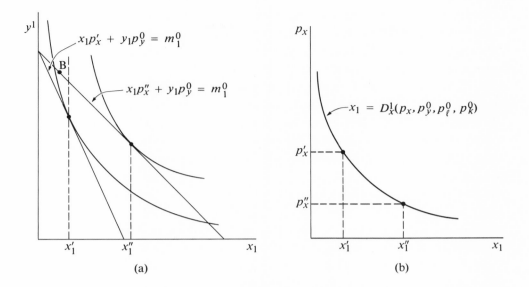

Fig. 3-4. Geometric derivation of person 1's demand curve from utility maximization

completely characterized by tangencies between indifference surfaces and budget planes, under such an interpretation demand and supply functions (3.3-1) can often be found by solving (3.2-3), (3.2-5), and (3.2-6) (with the naughts on x_1, y_1, and z_1 removed) for x_1, y_1, and z_1 as functions of p_x, p_y, p_ℓ, and p_k. (The π_x and π_y in (3.2-3) are eliminated because they, too, are functions of prices.) Regardless, α, β_1, and $\bar{k}_1$ do not modify with price alterations and are parameters implicit in D_x^1, D_y^1, and S_ℓ^1. Before exploring the implications of this interpretation, however, it is worth going back to some geometry.

Let p_y, p_ℓ, and p_k be set at specific values p_y^0, p_ℓ^0, and p_k^0, respectively. Then person 1's demand function for good x reduces to a two-variable relation

$$x_1 = D_x^1(p_x, p_y^0, p_\ell^0, p_k^0), \qquad (3.3\text{-}3)$$

which is shown as a demand curve in figure 3-4(b). (In consequence of the discussion at the start of sec. 2.2, the dependent variable has been placed on the horizontal axis and the independent variable on the vertical axis.) If person 1's utility function were such that as p_x varies, the utility-maximizing value of z_1 never changes (perhaps $z_1 = z_1^0$), then utility maximization may always be pictured as in figure 3-3(b) with an unchanging "partial" indifference map. Alternatively, a diagram like figure 3-3(b) would also apply if z_1 were dropped as an argument of the utility function, leaving the complete indifference map confined to the x_1-y_1 plane. Of course, a fixed value of z_1 or ℓ_1 would now have to be chosen "arbitrarily" (again write $z_1 = z_1^0$) rather than by maximization. (Such an approach is taken in chap. 6.) In both cases, suppose $\beta_1(\pi_x + \pi_y) = 0$ so that person 1's income does not modify with alterations in p_x. Then under either pair of conditions, the demand curve of figure 3-4(b) may be geometrically derived from the appropriate two-dimensional indifference map in the following way: Choose $p_x = p_x'$, say, in figure 3-4(b). Given values p_y^0, p_ℓ^0, p_k^0, and z_1^0, the budget constraint (3.2-3) becomes (as in (3.2-4)) the line

$$x_1 p_x' + y_1 p_y^0 = m_1^0,$$

where p_x', p_y^0, and m_1^0 (from (3.2-2)) are specific numbers. Plotting the budget line in figure 3-4(a), utility is seen to be maximized at a basket which contains $x_1 = x_1'$. This furnishes the x_1 coordinate associated with p_x' on the demand curve in figure 3-4(b). Repeating the construction for all positive values of p_x (with p_y^0, p_ℓ^0, p_k^0, and z_1^0 remaining fixed) yields the demand curve. Thus if $p_x = p_x''$, utility maximization requires that x_1'' be demanded. Of course, if z_1^0 were permitted to vary with changes in p_x (as it generally does when person 1 maximizes $U^1(x_1, y_1, z_1)$ subject to (3.3-2)), then a different demand curve would obtain. The indifference curve from which x_1'' emerges in figure 3-4(a) would be taken from a different partial indifference map than the one that results in x_1'.

A parallel construction yields person 1's supply curve for labor time under similar assumptions about his utility function, the vanishing of $\beta_1(\pi_x + \pi_y)$, and the fixity of p_x, p_y, p_k, and, say, y_1. An indifference curve diagram depicting maximization for this situation appears in figure 3-5. With $p_x = p_x^0$, $p_y = p_y^0$,

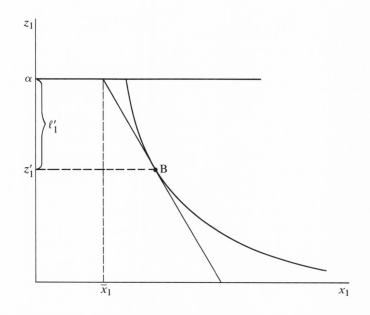

Fig. 3-5. Determination of person 1's supply of labor from utility maximization

$p_k = p_k^0$, $y_1 = y_1^0$, and, for example, $p_\ell = p_\ell'$, the equation of the budget line in that diagram appears as

$$x_1 p_x^0 + z_1 p_\ell' = \alpha p_\ell' + \bar{k}_1 p_k^0 - y_1^0 p_y^0.$$

Along this budget line, if person 1 were to spend all time at leisure so that $z_1 = \alpha$ and $\ell_1 = \alpha - z_1 = 0$, his income after capital purchases (saving) would still be sufficient to permit the purchase of $\bar{x}_1$. In the utility-maximizing basket (at point B in the diagram), $z_1 = z_1'$ and hence $\ell_1 = \alpha - z_1'$.

Returning to the general demand and supply functions of (3.3-1), it is important to point out that interpreting them as the outcome of constrained utility maximization by the consumer imposes significant restrictions on their character. This is because nontrivial properties must be prescribed for the utility function in order to be able to perform the maximization, and these properties force the utility maximizing baskets to have traits such as those described in section 3.2. To illustrate, since utility maximizing baskets cannot lie on any of the coordinate planes that bound the commodity space, the function values of D_x^1 and D_y^1 are always positive, while that of S_ℓ^1 is always less than α. Furthermore, since utility maximizing baskets must lie on the budget plane, one of D_x^1, D_y^1, and S_ℓ^1 can always be derived from the other two by substitution of $z_1 = \alpha - \ell_1$ and then (3.3-1) into the budget constraint (3.2-3). And lastly, because multiplying all market prices by the same positive number λ (for example, 2) multiplies π_x and π_y by λ, and hence has no effect on the budget constraint,[5] and because this change also does not modify person 1's indifference map, the utility maximizing basket is the same both before and after the multiplication. Thus

$$D_x^1(\lambda p_x, \lambda p_y, \lambda p_\ell, \lambda p_k) = D_x^1(p_x, p_y, p_\ell, p_k), \qquad (3.3\text{-}4)$$

and a similar result holds for D_y^1 and S_ℓ^1.

There are still further implications of utility maximization. But in spite of the picture economists almost universally employ to depict consumer demand curves (e.g., fig. 3-4(b)), one thing that the assumptions of sections 3.1 and 3.2 do not imply is that demand curves derived from equations like (3.3-3) necessarily slope downward. For regardless of whether z_1 is fixed at z_1^0 as p_x varies, the demand curve in figure 3-4(b) slopes downward between p_x' and p_x'' because the tangency that produces x_1'' lies to the right of that yielding x_1' in figure 3-4(a). But if the tangency producing x_1'' were to be located, instead, to the left of the one that provides x_1'—say, at point B in figure 3-4(a) (an eventuality not precluded by anything posited thus far)—then the demand curve in figure 3-4(b) would slope upward between p_x' and p_x''. In analogous fashion, the labor-time supply curve could slope either upward or downward depending on the relative location of the tangencies in figure 3-5 as p_ℓ modulates.

Still, it is clear that the explanation of consumer demand and supply functions given here cannot be applied to all possible

---

5. For example, multiplication of all price values by λ does not change the profit-maximizing values of x, ℓ_x, and k_x. Hence, according to (5.1-2), π_x is multiplied by λ.

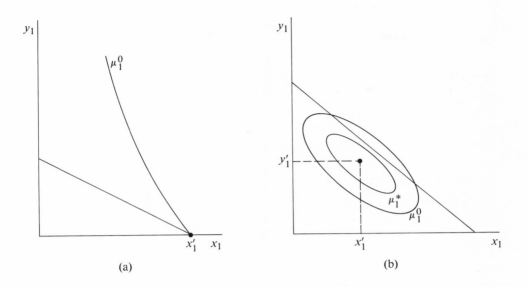

Fig. 3-6. Weakening the assumptions imposed on the utility function

candidates for such functions, because some will not satisfy the restrictions imposed by constrained utility maximization as described, in part, above. Although subsequent discussion considers only those demand and supply functions for which the above explanation is relevant, the reader should be aware that this class of explainable functions can be expanded by weakening the assumptions imposed. For example, the requirement that interior indifference surfaces not touch the coordinate planes of the commodity space could be dropped, thus permitting "corner" maxima such as $(x_1', 0)$ in figure 3-6(a) (which is again drawn for z_1 fixed at some z_1^0). It would then become possible for $x_1 = 0$, $y_1 = 0$, and $\ell_1 = \alpha$ to be (not necessarily simultaneous) function values of D_x^1, D_y^1, and S_ℓ^1, respectively. One might, in addition, also weaken the assumptions that a larger basket of commodities is always preferred to a smaller basket and that indifference surfaces be strictly convex, in order to allow for utility functions with global maxima as drawn in figure 3-6(b) (also under the supposition that $z_1 = z_1^0$). Here $\mu_1^* > \mu_1^0$, and the greatest utility obtainable in the x_1-y_1 plane is at (x_1', y_1'). With the budget line shown in figure 3-6(b), utility is maximized (with respect to x_1 and y_1) over the budget set at (x_1', y_1'), a basket which does not lie on the budget line. Hence for price values that yield such situations, one of D_x^1, D_y^1, or S_ℓ^1 can no longer be derived from the others by using the budget constraint (3.2-3). In both of these cases, weakening the original assumptions expands the collection of functions that are explainable by reducing the severity of the restraints imposed on demand and supply functions generated by constrained utility maximization.

To summarize the argument of this chapter, assume that the consumer possesses preferences and indifferences that can be represented by a continuous (ordinal) utility function whose marginal utilities are calculable, whose interior indifference surfaces are strictly convex and avoid the coordinate planes that bound the commodity space, and for which a larger basket of commodities is always preferred to a smaller one. Suppose also that the consumer never spends more than he (or she) earns, and that he always chooses quantities of final goods to buy and quantities of factors (i.e., labor time) to sell by maximizing utility subject to his budget constraint. Then this consumer's demand and supply functions (i.e., his market behavior) having certain properties are implied. These functions are taken to be those listed at the beginning of the chapter (omitting S_k^1 and S_k^2) and are the ones employed to obtain the appropriate market functions in section 2.1. Thus, although there is no guarantee that the consumer is, in fact, a utility maximizer, the model constructed here and the vision from which it emanates explains his behavior as if he were. The argument itself, which has been developed primarily with respect to person 1, applies without modification to person 2. Of course the sum of the fractions of profits $\pi_x + \pi_y$ returned to persons 1 and 2 is unity, that is, $\beta_1 + \beta_2 = 1$.

4 Production and Cost

Before proceeding to explain individual firm behavior as such, it is convenient to begin with some conceptual matters that set the stage for what is to come. As described in section 1.1, the firm converts inputs into output according to a given technology (i.e., the collection of all available information relating to the ways in which inputs may be combined to produce output). Its options for production are summarized in its production function (defined below). These options not only furnish a range of output levels for the firm but also provide a variety of alternatives for producing every (level of) output. Once the market prices of inputs are specified, the cost of all options is determined. Of course, for any output, the cost of some methods of production is less than others. The cost of the cheapest way of producing an output is usually singled out as *the* cost of that output, and the function that associates this latter cost to each output is the firm's cost function. The main concern of the present chapter is with the relationship between the cost and production functions of the firm. In this discussion, production functions are considered first, followed by cost minimization and then long- and short-run cost functions. Significant pieces of the presentation have analogous counterparts in the model of consumer behavior in chapter 3 and these are identified where appropriate. As was done with persons, only the case of one of the firms, namely the firm that produces x (or just firm x), is described. The exact same discussion applies to firm y.

The relevant space for analyzing firm x is the input space

$$\{(\ell_x, k_x): \ell_x \geq 0, k_x \geq 0\},$$

where (ℓ_x, k_x) is a basket of inputs consisting of ℓ_x units of labor (i.e., labor time) and k_x units of old capital (i.e., capital services). The production function of firm x, written

$$x = F^x(\ell_x, k_x),$$

indicates the maximum output x that can be produced from each basket of inputs (ℓ_x, k_x), given technology. It determines a surface in three dimensions, a finite portion of which is illustrated in figure 4-1. (The production function depicted in figure 4-1 is strictly concave, that is, any straight line segment connecting two distinct positive outputs on the production surface lies, except for end points, entirely below that surface.) Although not having the property of ordinality, the production function still plays much the same role in thinking about the firm as the utility function does when dealing with the consumer. Like the utility function, the production function is another basic element in the Walrasian vision.

Let $x^0 = F^x(\ell_x^0, k_x^0)$ where $\ell_x^0 > 0$ and $k_x^0 > 0$. In parallel with the notion of indifference surface, the isoquant through (ℓ_x^0, k_x^0) or the x^0 isoquant is the set of all input baskets in the input space yielding the same output x^0:

$$\left\{(\ell_x, k_x): F^x(\ell_x, k_x) = x^0\right\}.$$

Because there are only two inputs, isoquants are pictured as curves in the nonnegative quadrant of the two-dimensional input plane. (Recall that indifference curves could be obtained from indifference surfaces only by fixing the value assigned to one of the three commodities appearing in the utility function. Furthermore, different indifference curves arose depending on which good was held fixed and at which value.) The collection of all isoquants is the isoquant map.

Typically, the analysis of the firm is approached from two perspectives concerning input variation. On one hand, both

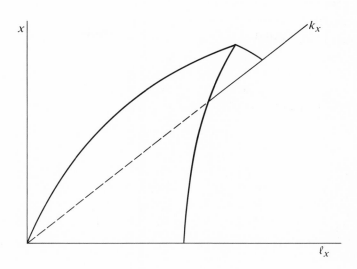

Fig. 4-1. Strictly concave production function

(old) capital and labor are allowed to modify; on the other, only labor may change. These situations are referred to as the long run and the short run, respectively. Thus the production function introduced above is long run in character. The short-run production function is secured from the long-run production function by setting $k_x = \bar{k}_x$, where $\bar{k}_x$ is a fixed number:

$$x = F^x(\ell_x, \bar{k}_x).$$

The short-run production function is the production function for firm x with plant size (as determined by) $\bar{k}_x$. Using the terminology long run and short run is suggestive of time. Indeed, the long run is sometimes described as a period of time sufficiently long so that both capital and labor may be varied in production, while the short run is short enough so that although labor may be varied, capital cannot. But evidently, the distinction between the long run and the short run has more to do with the specification of which inputs in the model are variable than it does with actual periods of time.

Another way to view the short-run production function is as a total product function. There are two such functions: that with respect to labor, TP_ℓ^x, is defined as

$$TP_\ell^x(\ell_x) = F^x(\ell_x, \bar{k}_x), \qquad (4.1\text{-}1)$$

while that with respect to capital is

$$TP_k^x(k_x) = F^x(\bar{\ell}_x, k_x),$$

where $\bar{\ell}_x$ and $\bar{k}_x$ are fixed. In other words, $TP_k^x(k_x)$ is a function of the single variable k_x. It is a section of the production function found by holding ℓ_x at $\bar{\ell}_x$ and altering k_x. Modification in $\bar{\ell}_x$ necessarily changes TP_k^x. Similar comments apply to TP_ℓ^x, which is also the short-run production function for a given plant size.

Consider, for a moment, $TP_\ell^x(\ell_x)$ with $k_x = \bar{k}_x > 0$. The average product of labor (per unit of labor input) is found from

$$AP_\ell^x(\ell_x) = \frac{TP_\ell^x(\ell_x)}{\ell_x},$$

at each value of $\ell_x > 0$. The marginal product at positive ℓ_x^0 (and $\bar{k}_x$)—like marginal utility—has two forms. It may be expressed approximately as

$$MP_\ell^x(\ell_x^0) = \frac{TP_\ell^x(\ell_x^0 + \Delta\ell_x) - TP_\ell^x(\ell_x^0)}{\Delta\ell_x},$$

where $\Delta\ell_x$ is a small number, or exactly as the derivative

$$MP_\ell^x(\ell_x^0) = \lim_{\Delta\ell_x \to 0} \frac{TP_\ell^x(\ell_x^0 + \Delta\ell_x) - TP_\ell^x(\ell_x^0)}{\Delta\ell_x}.$$

As in the case of the consumer, both forms are used interchangeably without distinction in subsequent discussion. An example of a total product curve for labor together with the average and marginal product curves it implies is drawn for $k_x = \bar{k}_x$ in figure 4-2. Notice that $MP_\ell^x(\ell_x) = 0$ where TP_ℓ^x has a maximum ($\ell_x = \ell_x'$), that MP_ℓ^x has a maximum where TP_ℓ^x

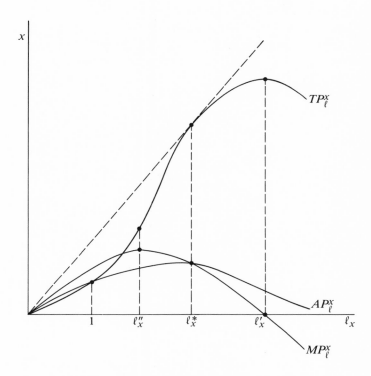

Fig. 4-2. Total, average, and marginal product curves

has an inflection point ($\ell_x = \ell_x''$), that AP_ℓ^x has a maximum where TP_ℓ^x is tangent to a ray from the origin ($\ell_x = \ell_x^*$), that MP_ℓ^x intersects AP_ℓ^x from above where AP_ℓ^x has its maximum ($\ell_x = \ell_x^*$), and that AP_ℓ^x intersects TP_ℓ^x from above at $\ell_x = 1$. Implicitly, scales measuring average and marginal quantities have been superimposed on the x axis in figure 4-2.

The average product of capital AP_k^x and the marginal product of capital MP_k^x are defined analogously. Moreover, at any interior basket of the input space (i.e., one for which $\ell_x > 0$ and $k_x > 0$) the ratio of marginal products

$$\frac{MP_\ell^x(\ell_x)}{MP_k^x(k_x)},$$

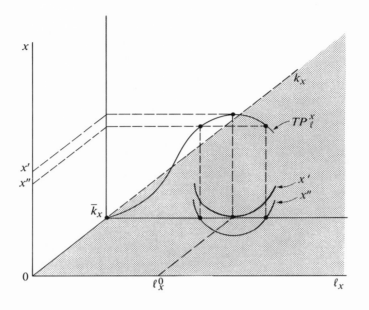

Fig. 4-3. Total product curve and isoquants

is called the marginal rate of technical substitution and, in parallel
with the situation for indifference curves, the negative of this
ratio is the slope of the isoquant through (ℓ_x, k_x) at (ℓ_x, k_x).

Now suppose that (unlike figure 4-1) the production function
F^x is shaped so that all of its total production curves, with
respect to both labor and capital, look like TP_ℓ^x in figure 4-2.
Then a typical relationship between isoquants and total product
curves is depicted in figure 4-3. The TP_ℓ^x curve in figure 4-3
is drawn in the "ℓ_x-x plane" with origin at $\bar{k}_x$, that is, in the
plane perpendicular to the k_x axis at $\bar{k}$. The x' and x'' isoquants
appear in the shaded ℓ_x-k_x plane. The x' isoquant corresponds
to a higher output than the x'' isoquant and is tangent at $(\ell_x^0, \bar{k}_x)$
to the ℓ_x axis of the ℓ_x-x plane through $\bar{k}_x$. It is the "highest"
isoquant attainable from this TP_ℓ^x curve since x' is the maximum
output achieved when $k_x = \bar{k}_x$. Likewise, the x' isoquant would
be tangent to an appropriate "k_x axis" where the TP_k^x curve over
that axis (ℓ_x being fixed) has a maximum.

Putting these isoquant-axis tangencies from all interior isoquants together in the long-run context (when both ℓ_x and k_x vary) yields ridge lines. The lower ridge line, then, is the collection of all interior input baskets at which an isoquant is tangent to an ℓ_x axis, or at which a TP_ℓ^x curve has a maximum as labor varies with capital held fixed:

$$\{(\ell_x, k_x): MP_\ell^x(\ell_x) = 0 \text{ and } k_x > 0\}.$$

The upper ridge line is the set of interior baskets for which a TP_k^x curve has a maximum as k_x modulates with ℓ_x fixed:

$$\{(\ell_x, k_x): MP_k^x(k_x) = 0 \text{ and } \ell_x > 0\}.$$

Since between the ridge lines both $MP_\ell^x(\ell_x) > 0$ and $MP_k^x(k_x) > 0$ in the present example, and since the slope along any isoquant is the negative of the ratio of MP_ℓ^x to MP_k^x, at each (ℓ_x, k_x) between the ridge lines the isoquant through (ℓ_x, k_x) is downward sloping at (ℓ_x, k_x). The ridge lines emerging from the production function generating figure 4-3, together with the x' isoquant, might appear as shown in figure 4-4.

Clearly, in producing output, the firm should employ baskets of inputs that lie between the ridge lines. Any output for which production is attempted with a basket positioned beyond this region can always be produced by a smaller basket that falls within it. Thus the area between the ridge lines is the only part of the input space that the firm need consider.

There are, however, production functions that do not have ridge lines. For example, the strictly concave function

$$F^x(\ell_x, k_x) = (\ell_x k_x)^{\frac{1}{4}},$$

which when graphed looks something like figure 4-1, has total product curves and isoquants as drawn, respectively, in figures 4-5(a) and 4-5(b). The isoquant in figure 4-5(b) runs off asymptotically to the ℓ_x and k_x axes. Here ridge lines cannot be defined as described above (although it is possible to think of them as degenerating into the ℓ_x and k_x axes), and the relevant region

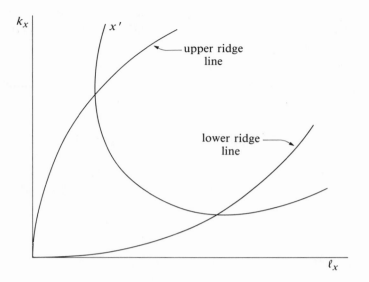

Fig. 4-4. Isoquant and ridge lines

of the input space commanding the firm's attention remains the entire positive quadrant of the ℓ_x-k_x plane.

Having discussed the technological conversion of inputs into outputs in the form of the production function, total product functions, isoquants, and ridge lines, the next step is to translate this information into cost data for the firm. To do so requires the introduction of input prices and the idea of cost minimization subject to constraint. The present section focuses on the long-run situation in which both labor and (old) capital inputs are variable.

4.2 Cost Minimization: The Long Run

Now firm x's cost, c_x, of input basket (ℓ_x, k_x) is

$$c_x = \ell_x p_\ell + k_x p_k, \qquad (4.2\text{-}1)$$

where p_ℓ is the price of labor and p_k is the price (rental) of capital. As usual, input price values are determined in the economy's markets and firms regard them as given parameters which cannot be controlled. Note the similarity between the form

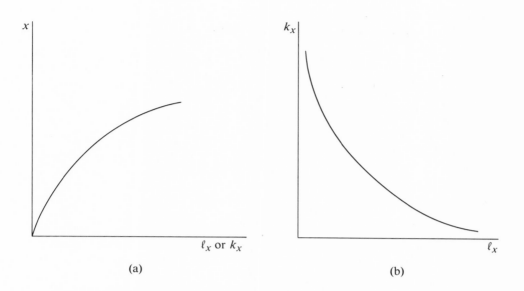

ℓ_x or k_x

(a)

ℓ_x

(b)

Fig. 4-5. Total product curve and isoquant for a strictly concave production function

of (4.2-1) and that of person 1's budget constraint for z_1 fixed in equation (3.2-4). Indeed, for a specified c_x, the graph of (4.2-1) in the ℓ_x-k_x plane looks exactly like the picture of (3.2-4) in figure 3-3(b) except that its slope is $-p_\ell/p_k$, instead of $-p_x/p_y$, and its vertical and horizontal intercepts are, respectively, c_x/p_k and c_x/p_ℓ, instead of m_1^0/p_y and m_1^0/p_x. This graph is an isocost line: it depicts the collection of all input baskets having identical cost c_x, given input prices p_ℓ and p_k. The set of all isocost lines as c_x varies (p_ℓ and p_k remaining constant) is the isocost map.

Let firm x be either the case of figures 4-1 and 4-5, or the case of figures 4-3 and 4-4. (Recall that the latter situation has ridge lines; the former does not.) Consider any output, say $x = x^0 > 0$. If the firm were to employ inputs so as to produce x^0 in the cheapest way (i.e., so as to minimize cost), then it would hire basket (ℓ_x^0, k_x^0) located at the tangency between an isocost line and the x^0 isoquant. This is drawn without ridge lines in figure 4-6. (If the x^0 isoquant were extended and ridge lines added, then the cost-minimizing basket, (ℓ_x^0, k_x^0), would lie between them.) Observe that x^0 may be thought

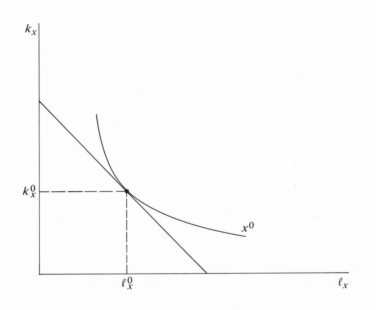

Fig. 4-6. Cost minimization subject to a given isoquant (output)

of as defining a constraining isoquant against which the firm is minimizing cost. Also, figure 4-6 is the same as figure 3-3(b) (describing utility maximization subject to the budget constraint) with appropriate adjustments in the names of curves and variables. The reader should not be fooled by the substitution of constrained minimization for constrained maximization: for it is also possible to think of the consumer as choosing baskets of final goods by minimizing "expenditure" subject to a fixed level of utility.

Analogous to the analysis of the consumer, part of the mathematical statement of the tangency in figure 4-6 is that the marginal rate of technical substitution (the negative of the slope of the isoquant) at (ℓ_x^0, k_x^0) equals the input price ratio:

$$\frac{MP_\ell^x(\ell_x^0)}{MP_k^x(k_x^0)} = \frac{p_\ell}{p_k},$$

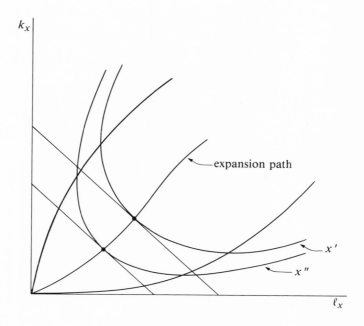

Fig. 4-7. Expansion path

or equivalently,[1] that

$$\frac{MP_\ell^x(\ell_x^0)}{p_\ell} = \frac{MP_k^x(k_x^0)}{p_k}.$$

This equation, together with the long-run production function $x^0 = F^x(\ell_x^0, k_x^0)$, completely characterizes all cost-minimizing baskets (ℓ_x^0, k_x^0) between the ridge lines as x^0 varies, for all values of p_ℓ and p_k.

Now fix p_ℓ and p_k at specific values. Then the expansion path, given those specific values for p_ℓ and p_k, is precisely the collection of all such cost-minimizing baskets between the ridge lines as x^0 modulates over all potential outputs. It is shown with ridge lines and two isoquants in figure 4-7. (Notice that the isocost line tangent to the x' isoquant is parallel to that tangent to the x'' isoquant.) Thus, if it is to pursue cost

---

1. As is the case with (3.2-7), the meaning of the ratios in the following equation necessarily stands in relation to some appropriately chosen normalization of prices.

minimization, the relevant region of the input space that the firm has to consider shrinks from the entire area between the ridge lines to the expansion path. (For this reason, subsequent isoquant diagrams for firm x do not need to depict ridge lines even when they exist, and hence these lines are often omitted below.)

Whereas utility maximization subject to the budget constraint is the basis for explaining consumer demand and supply functions in chapter 3, its counterpart in the analysis of the firm, namely cost minimization subject to an isoquant, serves to define cost as a function of output. It is here that the close analogy between Walrasian models of the consumer and firm end.

4.3 Long-Run Cost Functions

Let p_ℓ and p_k be given by the markets and let $x^0 > 0$ be a potential output for firm x. Then the cost of output x^0 is described as the cost of the least-cost (i.e., cost-minimizing) basket of inputs for producing x^0. Furthermore, the long-run total cost function is written

$$c_x = LRTC^x(x),$$

where c_x is the cost of x for each x, and $LRTC^x$ is the symbolic name of the function. To geometrically derive the long-run total cost curve (i.e., the graph of $LRTC^x$), choose an x^0 on the x axis in figure 4-8(a). Then x^0 identifies an isoquant in the input space of figure 4-8(b). Since p_ℓ and p_k have been specified, the slope of the relevant isocost lines and hence the tangency between the x^0 isoquant and an isocost line at some (ℓ_x^0, k_x^0) is determined (fig. 4-8(b)). The cost of x^0 is then plotted as

$$c_x^0 = \ell_x^0 p_\ell + k_x^0 p_k$$

in figure 4-8(a). Thus the long-run total cost function (and curve) is defined with respect to input baskets on the expansion path. Each change in p_ℓ or p_k transforms the expansion path and, along with it, the $LRTC^x$ function (and curve) as well.

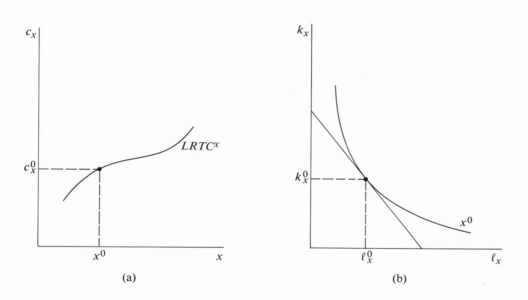

Fig. 4-8. Geometric derivation of the long-run total cost curve

Long-run average and marginal costs are obtained in the usual way. The former is given by

$$LRAC^x(x) = \frac{LRTC^x(x)}{x},$$

while the latter is characterized either as

$$LRMC^x(x) = \frac{LRTC^x(x + \Delta x) - LRTC^x(x)}{\Delta x},$$

where Δx is a small number, or as

$$LRMC^x(x) = \lim_{\Delta x \to 0} \frac{LRTC^x(x + \Delta x) - LRTC^x(x)}{\Delta x}.$$

These definitions apply only to outputs x that are positive.

A common long-run total cost curve and the long-run average and marginal cost curves derived from it appear in figure 4-9. The properties of this diagram parallel, in part, those of figure 4-2: First, $LRMC^x$ has a minimum where $LRTC^x$ has an

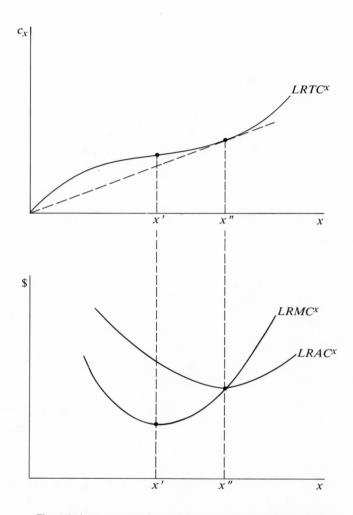

Fig. 4-9. Long-run total, average, and marginal cost curves

inflection point ($x = x'$). Second, $LRAC^x$ has a minimum where $LRTC^x$ is tangent to a ray from the origin ($x = x''$). Third, at the same $x = x''$, $LRMC^x$ crosses $LRAC^x$ from below. Note that both average and marginal quantities are measured along the vertical axis in the lower graph.

4.4 Cost in the Short Run

Recall that in the short run, labor input is variable but capital input is fixed. With $k_x = \bar{k}_x > 0$, the short-run production function is

$$x = F^x(\ell_x, \bar{k}_x), \qquad (4.4\text{-}1)$$

and the firm is said to have a plant size of $\bar{k}_x$.

The short-run cost of an output x may be split into two parts. Total fixed cost, TFC^x, is the cost of the fixed input needed to produce x, or

$$TFC^x(x) = \bar{k}_x p_k.$$

This, of course, remains constant even as x varies. The total variable cost, TVC^x, is the cost of the variable input in the production of x. The quantity of the variable input may be determined from equation (4.4-1) since both x (the output level) and $\bar{k}_x$ are known. Pictorially, with the firm restricted to the line $k_x = \bar{k}_x$ in figure 4-10, the quantity of labor required to produce x is found at the intersection of the x isoquant and the line $k_x = \bar{k}_x$. Such variable input is the "least-cost" way of producing x in the sense that, under present conditions, it is the only way of producing x. Thus

$$TVC^x(x) = \ell_x p_\ell,$$

where ℓ_x is the solution of (4.1-1) given the values of x and $\bar{k}_x$. The short-run cost of producing x is the sum of the fixed and variable costs:

$$SRTC^x(x) = TVC^x(x) + TFC^x(x). \qquad (4.4\text{-}2)$$

Clearly, these cost functions apply to a firm with plant size $\bar{k}_x$. Any modification in $\bar{k}_x$, p_ℓ, or p_k implies alterations in them.

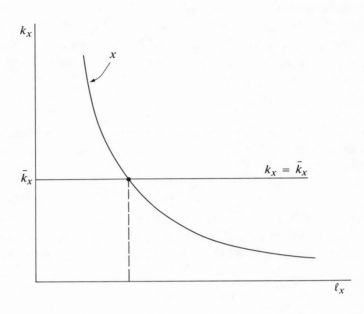

Fig. 4-10. Determination of labor input, given output, in the short run

As before, short-run average cost, average variable cost, average fixed cost, and short-run marginal cost are defined by, respectively,

$$SRAC^x(x) = \frac{SRTC^x(x)}{x},$$

$$AVC^x(x) = \frac{TVC^x(x)}{x},$$

$$AFC^x(x) = \frac{TFC^x(x)}{x},$$

and

$$SRMC^x(x) = \frac{SRTC^x(x + \Delta x) - SRTC^x(x)}{\Delta x},$$

for small Δx, or

$$SRMC^x(x) = \lim_{\Delta x \to 0} \frac{SRTC^x(x + \Delta x) - SRTC^x(x)}{\Delta x}.$$

Note that from (4.4-2),

$$SRAC^x(x) = AVC^x(x) + AFC^x(x), \qquad (4.4\text{-}3)$$

and that, since TFC^x is a constant function, the same marginal cost could be calculated using TVC^x instead of $SRTC^x$.

The analogue of figure 4-9 for short-run cost curves is depicted in figure 4-11. The shape of $SRTC^x$ is given and everything else is derived from it. The TFC^x and AFC^x curves are not shown. (The former is a line parallel to the x axis through the point $\bar{k}_x p_k$ on the c_x axis in the top graph, and the latter is a rectangular hyperbola through the point with coordinates $(1, \bar{k}_x p_k)$ in the bottom graph.) Because $SRTC^x$ and TVC^x have like slopes, one marginal curve, namely $SRMC^x$, applies to each and crosses both AVC^x and $SRAC^x$ at their respective minimum points. Although the same relationships in figure 4-9 between minimum points on the average and marginal curves in the lower graph and the total curves in the upper graph hold here, the minimum point on $SRAC^x$ is farther out on the x axis than that on AVC^x. Finally, $SRAC^x$ and AVC^x become closer together as x increases, reflecting (4.4-3) and the fact that AFC^x falls with rising x.

4.5 A Comparison of Long-Run and Short-Run Cost Curves

A basis for comparing long-run and short-run cost curves is provided in figure 4-12. Three outputs (isoquants) are considered: $x^* > x^0 > x''$. In the long run, as firm x expands its output from x'' to x^*, it moves along its expansion path. Suppose the firm's long-run total cost curve appears as drawn in figure 4-13(a). The short-run total cost curve for plant size $\bar{k}_x^0$ is shown in figure 4-13(a) as it might be read from figure 4-12. Clearly

$$SRTC^x(x'') > LRTC^x(x''),$$

because the basket employed to produce x'' in the long run (ℓ_x'', k_x'') is cost-minimizing, and hence the basket used in the short run with plant size $\bar{k}_x^0$, namely $(\ell_x', \bar{k}_x^0)$, must cost more. Likewise,

$$SRTC^x(x^0) = LRTC^x(x^0),$$

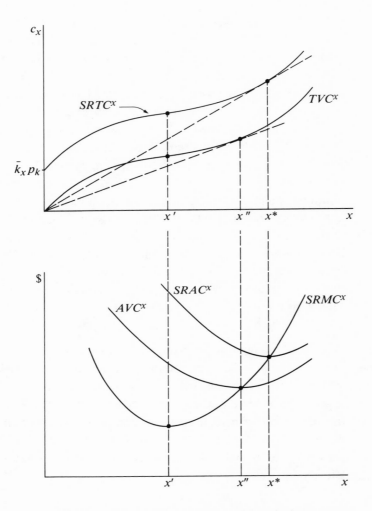

Fig. 4-11. Short-run total, average, and marginal cost curves

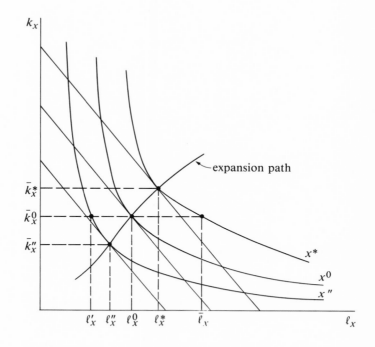

Fig. 4-12. Basis for comparing long-run and short-run cost curves

and

$$SRTC^x(x^*) > LRTC^x(x^*).$$

In figure 4-13(b), the $SRTC^x$ curves for plant sizes $\bar{k}_x''$ and $\bar{k}_x^*$ have been added to the picture of figure 4-13(a). Evidently, $LRTC^x(x)$ may be thought of as the minimum short-run total cost of producing x over all plant sizes $\bar{k}_x$, assuming input prices and technology (i.e., the production function) remain fixed.

The geometric relationship between $LRTC^x$ and various $SRTC^x$ curves, each drawn for a different plant size, is expressed in terms of average and marginal curves in figure 4-14. Output x^0 is the same as in figures 4-13(a) and 4-13(b), and only the short-run average cost curve for plant scale $\bar{k}_x^0$ is depicted. The facts that $SRAC^x$ lies everywhere above $LRAC^x$ except for the tangency at x^0, and that $SRMC^x$ cuts $LRMC^x$ from below

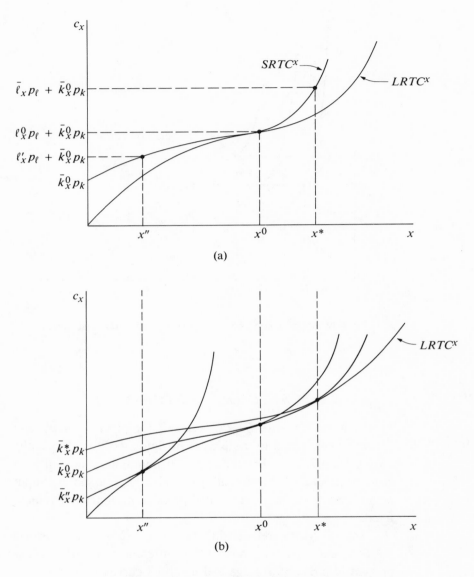

Fig. 4-13. Long-run and short-run total cost curves

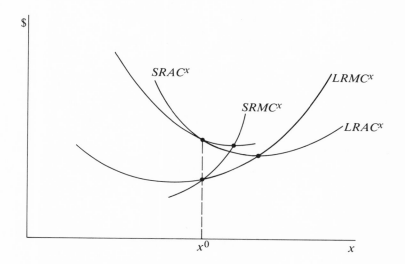

Fig. 4-14. Long-run and short-run average and marginal cost curves

over the same x^0 may be deduced from figure 4-13(a). Notice that only where $LRAC^x$ is at a minimum will it be tangent to some $SRAC^x$ curve at the latter's minimum point. As with $LRTC^x(x)$, each value of $LRAC^x(x)$ may be viewed as the minimum of the short-run average costs of producing x as plant size $\bar{k}_x$ varies over all possibilities.

It is not necessary that for all plant sizes the short-run total (or average) cost curve always be tangent to the long-run total (or, respectively, average) cost curve at exactly one point. If the firm's expansion path were to appear as in figure 4-15, for example, then only when $k_x = \bar{k}_x^0$ would $SRTC^x$ and $LRTC^x$ come together at a single point. For plant scales such as $\bar{k}_x''$, the short- and long-run total cost curves are tangent at two points, while for those like $\bar{k}_x^*$, they do not meet at all. In the last instance, $SRTC^x$ lies above $LRTC^x$ at all outputs.

Finally, the reader should remember that the entire discussion of this chapter applies exactly as it stands to the firm producing y with the symbol y replacing x in all places where the latter appears.

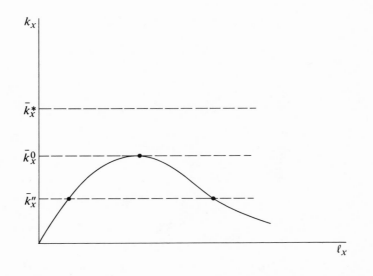

Fig. 4-15. Expansion path yielding short-run total cost curves that can be tangent to the long-run total cost curve at two points or not tangent at all

5   Individual Firm Behavior

Firms buy labor and rent previously produced (old) capital from consumers, using them to produce final consumption and new capital goods for sale to consumers. The buying and selling behavior by firms is encapsulated in their input demand and output supply functions. From section 2.1, those for firm x are

$$\ell_x = D_\ell^x(p_x, p_\ell, p_k),$$

$$k_x = D_k^x(p_x, p_\ell, p_k),$$

$$x = S^x(p_x, p_\ell, p_k),$$

and the functions describing firm y's behavior appear as

$$\ell_y = D_\ell^y(p_y, p_\ell, p_k),$$

$$k_y = D_k^y(p_y, p_\ell, p_k),$$

$$y = S^y(p_y, p_\ell, p_k).$$

To explain the source of these functions, attention now centers on construction of the third and last piece of the present Walrasian model. True to its Walrasian character, this piece, itself a model, assumes fixed technologies, that the buying and selling decisions of firms result from profit maximization, that firms regard market prices as beyond their influence, and that entry into each market is free. The last two suppositions, of course, relate to the perfect competitiveness of the economy's markets. Still further assumptions are introduced below. The practice of confining exposition to the case of a single firm, namely firm x, continues.

The chapter begins with a discussion of revenue and profit in section 5.1. The implications of profit maximization are examined in section 5.2. Sections 5.3 and 5.4 show how firm input demand and output supply functions emerge from profit maximization in the short and long run.

5.1 Revenue and Profit

Given a price for firm x's output, p_x, presented by the economy's markets, the total revenue received by the firm depends on output sold:

$$TR^x(x) = xp_x. \qquad (5.1\text{-}1)$$

Since p_x is constant (from the point of view of firm x), $TR^x(x)$ is a linear function of x. Average revenue is

$$AR^x(x) = \frac{TR^x(x)}{x} = p_x,$$

and marginal revenue, whether defined in approximate form as the additional revenue per unit obtained from the last increment of output sold, or in exact form as the derivative of TR^x, reduces to

$$MR^x(x) = p_x.$$

The profit accruing to firm x is the difference between its revenue and cost, or

$$\pi_x = xp_x - \ell_x p_\ell - k_x p_k, \qquad (5.1\text{-}2)$$

where π_x is the symbol denoting firm x's profit, and p_ℓ and p_k (in addition to p_x) have been given by the markets. Assume that in making its decisions the firm chooses x and ℓ_x, and in the long run k_x, so as to maximize π_x, and that such a maximization is performed against all configurations of p_x, p_ℓ, and p_k it faces. Clearly, since

$$\pi_x = xp_x - c_x,$$

where

$$c_x = \ell_x p_\ell + k_x p_k,$$

profit maximization necessarily implies that cost (c_x) is minimized subject to each level of output. Hence the construction of cost functions in chapter 4 applies. Long-run profit may therefore be written as

$$\pi_x = TR^x(x) - LRTC^x(x), \qquad (5.1\text{-}3)$$

and its short-run counterpart expressed (with k_x fixed at $\bar{k}_x$) as

$$\pi_x = TR^x(x) - SRTC^x(x), \qquad (5.1\text{-}4)$$

where TR^x is defined in (5.1-1).

As with utility maximization subject to the budget constraint, enough restrictions must be imposed to guarantee that firm x is usually able to maximize π_x, no matter what values of p_x, p_ℓ, and p_k the market delivers. The following assumptions suffice for present purposes. Take the production function to be such that

$$F^x(0,0) = 0,$$

and

$$F^x(\ell_x, k_x) \geq 0,$$

for all $\ell_x \geq 0$ and $k_x \geq 0$. Let F^x be continuous throughout the input space and let both marginal products be calculable (continuously, when expressed in derivative form) at every interior input basket. Suppose that a larger basket of inputs yields more output than a smaller one, that isoquants are strictly convex, and that these statements apply either to every input basket between the ridge lines or, when ridge lines do not exist, to every interior basket in the input space. In the latter case, suppose also that isoquants do not touch the ℓ_x and k_x axes. Lastly, assume that long- and short-run cost curves appear as drawn in figures 4-9, 4-11, and 4-13, so that marginal costs are computable (continuously, when expressed in derivative form) and marginal cost curves slope upward beyond appropriate output levels. (Similar requirements are made of firm y.)

It has already been suggested (sec. 1.2) that the notion of profit maximization is fundamental to the Walrasian vision. The implications of this assumption are considered next.

In the short-run situation with $k_x = \bar{k}_x$, the profit-maximizing output of firm x can be found by differentiating (5.1-4) with respect to x and equating this derivative to zero.[1] Thus output x^0 maximizes short-run profit if

5.2 Profit Maximization

$$MR^x(x^0) = SRMC^x(x^0),$$

or, in light of (5.1-1), if

$$SRMC^x(x^0) = p_x. \qquad (5.2\text{-}1)$$

In words, short-run profit is maximized where short-run marginal cost equals output price. Figure 5-1 illustrates the idea for a plant size of $\bar{k}_x$. Note that the symbol π^x (not π_x) is used to denote the profit curve in the diagram.[2] Furthermore, although there are two outputs such that marginal cost equals price, only at x^0, where marginal cost is rising, is profit maximized. Marginal cost is falling at x' and profit is at a minimum. To achieve profit maximization, then, not only does (5.2-1) have to be satisfied, but marginal cost must be rising as well. Observe that p_k, unlike p_ℓ, has no impact in determining x^0 in (5.2-1).

Once the profit-maximizing output (x^0) is known, the labor input required to produce that output (with plant size $\bar{k}_x$) is secured at the intersection of the x^0 isoquant and the line $k_x = \bar{k}_x$ in the input space (fig. 4-10 with x replaced by x^0). Assuming that the firm, like the consumer, demands and supplies only that which emerges from maximization, the quantities of labor input demanded and output supplied by firm x have now been determined for the particular p_x and p_ℓ given by the markets. The price of old capital is ignored since, in the present case, it is irrelevant to profit maximization. (Changes in p_k have

---

1. When short-run marginal cost is defined in approximate form, an alternative derivation leads to the same (in this case, approximate) result.

2. Under present notational conventions π^x would represent the entire profit function (or curve) of firm x, not just the (profit) function values π_x.

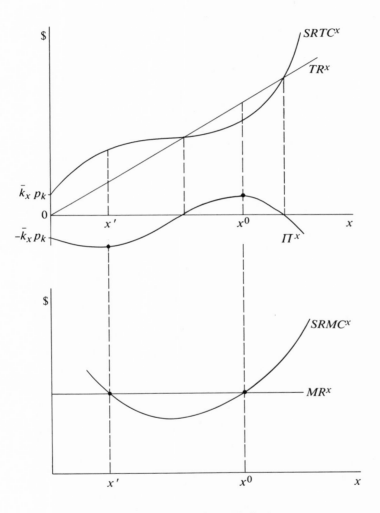

Fig. 5-1. Short-run profit maximization

the effect of shifting the short-run total cost and profit curves in fig. 5-1 vertically up or down; since the shapes of these curves remain unaltered, so does the profit-maximizing output x^0.) Hypothetical repetition of this procedure as p_x and p_ℓ vary both produces and explains the labor demand and output supply functions (as modified by the elimination of p_k) set out at the beginning of the chapter:

$$\ell_x = D_\ell^x(p_x, p_\ell),$$

$$x = S^x(p_x, p_\ell).$$

Since plant size is fixed in the short run, the firm's demand function for old capital is the constant function

$$\bar{k}_x = D_k^x(p_x, p_\ell, p_k).$$

Profit maximization in the long run using (5.1-3) yields a result similar to (5.2-1), namely,

$$LRMC^x(x^0) = p_x. \qquad (5.2-2)$$

With the appropriate relabeling of curves, figure 5-1 carries over to the long-run case, too, except that here the vertical intercepts of the $LRMC^x$ and π^x curves are zero. Moreover, knowing the profit-maximizing output (x^0) obtained from (5.2-2), the labor and capital inputs that go with it are found from the tangency of the x^0 isoquant with an isocost line whose slope is the negative of the ratio of the given input prices (fig. 4-8(b)). (The same labor inputs are also located at the intersection of the x^0 isoquant and the firm's expansion path.) Thus, in addition to output and labor input, long-run profit maximization also determines an "optimal" plant size. In the present case with profit-maximizing output x^0, denote the optimal plant size by k_x^0.

An alternate depiction of the determination of the optimal plant size is shown in figure 5-2. In this diagram the cost curves bear the same relationship to each other as they do in figure 4-14, only here the $SRAC^x$ curve is tangent to the $LRAC^x$ curve to the right of the latter's minimum point. (As with fig. 4-14, an isoquant diagram like fig. 4-12 could be drawn for fig. 5-2 to

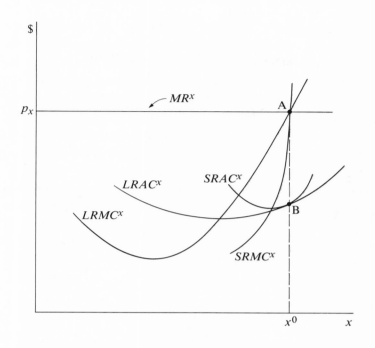

Fig. 5-2. Determination of the optimal plant size

demonstrate its derivation.) Both (5.2-1) and (5.2-2) are satisfied at point A:

$$LRMC^x(x^0) = SRMC^x(x^0) = p_x, \qquad (5.2\text{-}3)$$

and the firm finds itself at point B on its long-run average cost curve. But the firm does not actually produce from the $LRAC^x$ curve. For each point on that curve also lies on a $SRAC^x$ curve corresponding to a particular plant size. Once the optimal plant size is found, the firm knows the plant it needs. Then, operating with that plant and the associated short-run cost curves, it produces its long-run profit-maximizing output. Thus, the optimal plant size (k_x^0) is that associated with the $SRAC^x$ curve tangent to the $LRAC^x$ curve at B in figure 5-2.

Note also that long-run profit maximization, since it determines the optimal plant size k_x^0, implies short-run profit maximization with plant size k_x^0. The converse assertion, however, is not true. The firm can obviously maximize short-run profit with a nonoptimal plant size.

To summarize the long-run situation, firm x may be thought of as working through the following recipe in order to achieve profit maximization. Start with the entire input space. From the shape of the production function, locate ridge lines (if they are present) and exclude the area beyond them. Next, by introducing input prices and cost minimization, restrict attention still further to the expansion path. Express cost as a function of output, and then bring output price information and profit maximization to bear in determining the isoquant on which to operate. Lastly, the intersection of this isoquant and the expansion path identifies the input basket to hire. Hypothetically pursuing this recipe for all input and output prices dictated by the markets, and supposing that firm x always invokes long-run profit maximization to arrive at its buying and selling decisions, input demand and output supply functions are secured:

$$\ell_x = D_\ell^x(p_x, p_\ell, p_k),$$

$$k_x = D_k^x(p_x, p_\ell, p_k),$$

$$x = S^x(p_x, p_\ell, p_k).$$

However, to properly place these functions in the traditional long-run context requires some adjustments as described in section 5.4. Observe that the demand function for old capital is no longer a constant function as it was in the short-run circumstance, nor is the price of old capital irrelevant to the determination of ℓ_x and x.

5.3 Short-Run Demand and Supply Functions

Recall that accepting utility maximization subject to the budget constraint as the driving force behind consumer decision-making implies that the demand and supply functions representing consumer market behavior necessarily possess certain characteristics. The same is true for firms. Indeed, the price of capital has already been eliminated as an argument of the short-run D_ℓ^x and S^x functions. The intent of this section is to illustrate additional characteristics of the short-run input demand and output supply functions

$$\ell_x = D_\ell^x(p_x, p_\ell),$$

$$x = S^x(p_x, p_\ell),$$

$$\bar{k}_x = D_k^x(p_x, p_\ell, p_k),$$

derived from short-run profit maximization in section 5.2. (Remember that D_k^x is a constant function since plant size is fixed.)

With plant size specified at $k_x = \bar{k}_x$, and setting p_ℓ and p_k at constant levels p_ℓ^0 and p_k^0, consider short-run output supply as a function of p_x alone:

$$x = S^x(p_x, p_\ell^0). \qquad (5.3\text{-}1)$$

Then, subject to one qualification indicated below, the graph of (5.3-1) with the dependent variable on the horizontal axis and the independent variable on the vertical axis (recall sec. 2.2) or, in other words, the firm's supply curve, is the upward sloping portion of the $SRMC^x$ curve in figure 5-3. Indeed, equation (5.3-1) is nothing more than the inverse of

$$SRMC^x(x) = p_x,$$

where $p_\ell = p_\ell^0$ is implicit in $SRMC^x(x)$.

The qualification arises, however, because the firm has a further option that is not accounted for in the calculation of profit-maximizing outputs. Even though in figure 5-3 the firm is maximizing short-run profit at x' and x'' for respective prices p_x' and p_x'', it is still losing money. In these cases profit maximization means loss minimization. And when the minimum loss becomes too large, the firm can always close down. This means eliminating all labor input and reducing total variable cost to zero. Of course, since old capital (i.e., plant size) is fixed and cannot be changed in the short run, the firm must still absorb the fixed cost $\bar{k}_x p_k^0$ as a loss. Only when the revenue obtained by selling output remains larger than the cost of the variable input needed to produce that output, as it does when output price falls between the minimum values of $SRAC^x$ and AVC^x (for

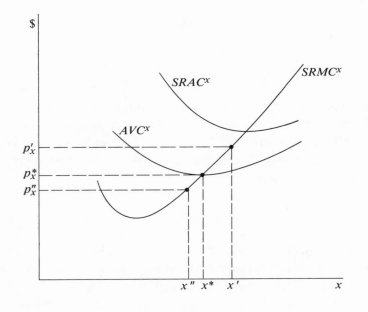

Fig. 5-3. Short-run supply curve of the firm

example, at p_x' in fig. 5-3), should firm x remain in operation. In such a situation

$$\pi_x > -\bar{k}_x p_k^0$$

at minimum-loss output. Otherwise, with p_x below the minimum value of AVC^x (for example, at p_x'' in fig. 5-3), firm x's losses are reduced by closing down.

With the above qualification in mind, let p_x^* represent a price equal to the minimum value of average variable cost. Denote the output whose average variable cost is that minimum by x^* (see fig. 5-3). Then the supply function (5.3-1) becomes

$$x = S^x(p_x, p_\ell^0),$$

where $x = 0$ when $p_x < p_x^*$, and x is determined from the firm's short-run marginal cost curve when $p_x \geq p_x^*$. (It is convenient to suppose that the firm stays open at the "shut-down" point $p_x = p_x^*$.) Furthermore, since the marginal cost curve slopes upward for all $x \geq x^*$, the firm's supply curve slopes upward for all $p_x \geq p_x^*$. (Recall that one could not infer a parallel property, i.e., downward sloping demand curves, in the case of the consumer.)

Just as marginal cost is related to the output supply function, so is marginal product linked to the labor demand function. To see how, substitute the short-run production function $x = F^x(\ell_x, \bar{k}_x)$ into the profit equation (5.1-2) with $k_x = \bar{k}_x$, so that

$$\pi_x = p_x F^x(\ell_x, \bar{k}_x) - \ell_x p_\ell - \bar{k}_x p_k.$$

Since the short-run production function is also the total product function $TP_\ell^x(\ell_x)$,

$$\pi_x = p_x TP_\ell^x(\ell_x) - \ell_x p_\ell - \bar{k}_x p_k.$$

Now if ℓ_x is selected so as to maximize π_x, then differentiating with respect to ℓ_x and equating the result to zero yields

$$p_x MP_\ell^x(\ell_x) = p_\ell. \qquad (5.3\text{-}2)$$

Again, the price of old capital does not figure in the determination of the profit-maximizing value of ℓ_x. The left-hand side of (5.3-2) is the value of the marginal product of labor at ℓ_x or, expressed in approximate terms, the additional revenue per unit that firm x receives upon hiring the last increment of labor. Maximization requires that the value of the marginal product of labor be equal to labor's wage (price).

To identify the firm's short-run labor demand as a function of the single variable p_ℓ, let $k_x = \bar{k}_x$, $p_x = p_x^0$, and $p_k = p_k^0$, and write

$$\ell_x = D_\ell^x(p_x^0, p_\ell). \qquad (5.3\text{-}3)$$

Then (5.3-3) is the inverse of (5.3-2) with p_x replaced by p_x^0, and the labor demand curve (the graph of (5.3-3) with the dependent variable on the horizontal axis and the independent variable on the vertical axis) is the firm's MP_ℓ^x curve with its ordinate values multiplied everywhere by p_x^0, that is, its value-of-marginal-product curve. This statement, too, needs qualification, since for p_ℓ such that the minimum value of AVC^x (which depends on p_ℓ) is larger than p_x^0, the firm shuts down and $\ell_x = 0$. Of course, with p_x^0 constant, the shape of the firm's labor demand curve is similar to that of its marginal product curve as illustrated, for example, in figure 4-2.

Return now to the input demand and output supply functions of firm x derived from the maximization of long-run profit in section 5.2:

$$\ell_x = D_\ell^x(p_x, p_\ell, p_k),$$

$$k_x = D_k^x(p_x, p_\ell, p_k), \qquad\qquad (5.4\text{-}1)$$

$$x = S^x(p_x, p_\ell, p_k).$$

5.4 Long-Run Demand and Supply Functions

As they stand, input demand and output supply curves generated by these functions can be interpreted (like short-run functions) in terms of value-of-marginal-product and marginal cost curves. Thus with $p_\ell = p_\ell^0$ and $p_k = p_k^0$, the graph of

$$x = S^x(p_x, p_\ell^0, p_k^0),$$

(where the dependent variable is on the horizontal axis and the independent variable is on the vertical axis) is partly the upward sloping portion of the long-run marginal cost curve above the minimum value of $LRAC^x$. Lacking fixed inputs and hence fixed cost, firm x would close at prices p_x below this minimum value. Likewise, setting $p_x = p_x^0$, $p_k = p_k^0$, and $k_x = k_x^0$, or requiring $p_x = p_x^0$, $p_\ell = p_\ell^0$, and $\ell_x = \ell_x^0$, the corresponding pictures of

$$\ell_x = D_\ell^x(p_x^0, p_\ell, p_k^0),$$

or respectively,

$$k_x = D_k^x(p_x^0, p_\ell^0, p_k),$$

are the appropriate portions of value-of-marginal-product curves. Indeed, in addition to the derivation of section 5.2, the first two equations of (5.4-1) may also be obtained (in parallel to the relationship between (5.3-3) and (5.3-2)) as the solution of the system

$$\frac{p_\ell}{p_x} = MP_\ell^x(\ell_x, k_x),$$

$$\frac{p_k}{p_x} = MP_k^x(\ell_x, k_x),$$

(5.4-2)

where the implicit k_x in MP_ℓ^x and the implicit ℓ_x in MP_k^x (recall equation (4.1-1)) are made explicit and permitted to vary. (When the input demand equations of (5.4-1) are secured in this way, the third equation of (5.4-1) is found by substituting the input demand equations into the production function F^x.)

Moreover, the input demand and output supply functions (5.4-1) have a property akin to one of the characteristics of consumer demand and supply functions (3.3-1) derived from utility maximization. To see what this is, note first that multiplying all market prices by the same positive number λ has no effect on the slope of the firm's isocost lines, and hence does not change the least-cost basket of inputs for producing any output. From the construction of the long-run cost function in section 4.2, however, the cost of producing every output is still multiplied by λ. Furthermore, according to equation (5.1-1), the revenue associated with every output is also multiplied by λ as is, from (5.1-2), the profit. But the multiplication of the profit of every output by the same number λ cannot alter the profit-maximizing output and input basket because it has no impact on the general shape of the firm's profit function. Therefore, as in (3.3-4),

$$D_\ell^x(\lambda p_x, \lambda p_\ell, \lambda p_k) = D_\ell^x(p_x, p_\ell, p_k),$$

(5.4-3)

and a similar assertion holds for D_k^x and S^x.

Although the input demand and output supply functions of (5.4-1) are significant and figure importantly in subsequent discussion, they are not, in the traditional sense, long-run functions. This is because, in addition to the preclusion of fixed inputs, the long run is commonly characterized as a circumstance in which, even after maximization, firm profit is zero. And nothing has been assumed thus far that ensures such a condition is met. For future reference, then, the functions of (5.4-1) are referred to as "pseudo-long-run" input demand and output supply functions.[3]

The usual assumption that brings long-run profit to zero is the market property of free entry, that is, that long-run movements in and out of markets are costless. The idea is that positive profits accruing to sellers (firms) induces the entry of additional capital (or firms) until, with the added supply it creates, market price drops sufficiently to eliminate all profit. (Negative profits cause existing capital or firms to leave.) The question of why firms should produce at all when no profits are obtained is tricky and may be handled by revising the model to include a "normal" profit, apart from π_x, as the return to the "money capital" that is needed to finance production, and that has been put up by the "owners" of the firms.[4] In the present context, even though there can only be one firm in each of the output markets, the proper long-run setting requires that profits still vanish as additional capital enters the existing firms.[5] A drawing of firm x in such a situation is provided by figure 5-4: long-run profit is both maximized and zero at $p_x = p_x^0$ and $x = x^0$.

In the long run, then, price is determined by the minimum value of $LRAC^x$. The latter, in turn, depends on the values of p_ℓ and p_k served up by the markets. Hence p_x cannot be an independent variable in the firm's long-run input demand and output supply functions. These functions, as derived from

---

3. By adding a third input, creating a market for it, and appropriately modifying budget constraints and other equations, these pseudo-long-run input demand and output supply functions could be viewed as short-run functions where the new input is taken to be the fixed input in production.

4. See, for example, D. W. Katzner, *Walrasian Microeconomics: An Introduction to the Economic Theory of Market Behavior* (Reading, Mass.: Addison-Wesley, 1988), chap. 12.

5. Recall the pedagogical device introduced in section 1.2 that each firm behaves as if it participated in perfectly competitive markets. Note also that, since the total quantity of old capital available for use in production is fixed, any capital entering one firm must have been taken from the other. This means that long-run adjustments to eliminate positive or negative firm profits could result in changes in the price of capital as well as, or in lieu of, the actual movement of capital itself.

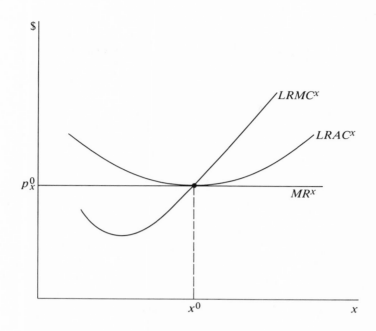

Fig. 5-4. Long-run profit maximization and free entry

long-run profit maximization and the free entry requirement, are written as

$$\ell_x = D_\ell^x(p_\ell, p_k),$$

$$k_x = D_k^x(p_\ell, p_k),$$

$$x = S^x(p_\ell, p_k).$$

Fixing $p_\ell = p_\ell^0$ and $p_k = p_k^0$, if one were to plot the long-run supply curve of firm x in the x-p_x plane, it would appear as the vertical straight line shown in figure 5-5, where x^0 is determined as in figure 5-4. Thus, upon introduction of demand into figure 5-5, if long-run market equilibrium were to be attained, then the market demand curve would have to intersect this vertical supply curve (recall that firm x is the only supplier in the market for x) at the level of firm x's minimum long-run average cost. Clearly, unlike the short-run and pseudo-long-run contexts, such a long-run supply curve cannot sensibly be interpreted in terms of the rising portion of the firm's long-run marginal cost curve.

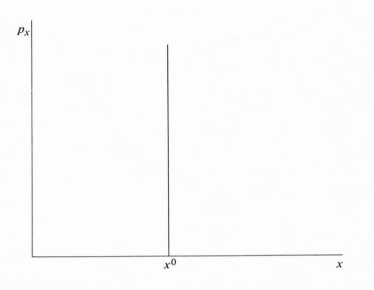

Fig. 5-5. Long-run supply curve of the firm with free entry

At this point, it is worth noting once again that all of the above carries over to firm y with the obvious modification in symbolic notation.

6   A Walrasian Model

Previous chapters have developed models of the operation of markets and of the behavior within them of both consumers and firms. The current task is to combine these pieces into a single Walrasian model of the entire economy and to examine some of its properties. The vision articulated by this model is described in chapter 7.

Three options are available. Specifically, the consumer demand and supply functions of chapter 3 could be combined with the short-run, the pseudo-long-run, or the long-run model of the firm (chap. 5) to obtain the market demand and supply functions of chapter 2. Although each of these three constructions has its own significance and peculiarities, only one can be considered here. The present purpose of articulating the Walrasian vision is best served by focusing attention on the Walrasian model secured in the pseudo-long-run case. For pedagogical reasons, one further simplifying restriction is added, namely, that (in addition to old capital) the quantity of labor time supplied by each consumer is fixed.

The chapter is divided into five parts. Section 6.1 provides a relatively complete list of the equations of the model and section 6.2 interprets the solution (equilibrium) of these equations in terms of economic reality. The optimality properties of this equilibrium are considered in section 6.3 and the question of whether it maximizes welfare is taken up in section 6.4. Section 6.5 is concerned with the existence and uniqueness of the equilibrium.

This section, in attempting to summarize earlier discussion, sets out the main equations of the pseudo-long-run Walrasian model, along with the assumptions that lie most directly behind them. For the sake of completeness, equations for both consumers and firms are provided, with those for person 2 and firm y largely appearing for the first time.

Let the fixed amounts of labor (i.e., labor time) supplied by persons 1 and 2 be $\bar{\ell}_1$ and $\bar{\ell}_2$, respectively. Then leisure (leisure time) must be consumed in the quantities

$$\bar{z}_1 = \alpha - \bar{\ell}_1,$$
$$\bar{z}_2 = \alpha - \bar{\ell}_2,$$

where α denotes total time available. Since z_1 and z_2 are no longer variables whose values have to be chosen by maximization, the utility functions representing the preferences of these individuals may exclude them as arguments (such a case was considered in sec. 3.3):

$$\mu_1 = U^1(x_1, y_1),$$
$$\mu_2 = U^2(x_2, y_2).$$

Each utility function is assumed to be continuous, with calculable marginal utilities (the latter are taken to be continuous when expressed in derivative form) and interior indifference curves that are strictly convex and do not touch the x and y axes of the relevant commodity space. Larger baskets of goods are taken to be preferred to smaller ones. Budget constraints are given by

$$x_1 p_x + y_1 p_y = \bar{\ell}_1 p_\ell + \bar{k}_1 p_k + \beta_1(\pi_x + \pi_y),$$
$$x_2 p_x + y_2 p_y = \bar{\ell}_2 p_\ell + \bar{k}_2 p_k + \beta_2(\pi_x + \pi_y),$$

$$(6.1\text{-}1)$$

where $\beta_1 + \beta_2 = 1$, and β_1 and β_2 are, respectively, the fractions of combined profit distributed to persons 1 and 2.

Choosing baskets so as to maximize utility subject to budget constraints leads to

$$\frac{MU_x^1(x_1, y_1)}{MU_y^1(x_1, y_1)} = \frac{p_x}{p_y},$$

$$\frac{MU_x^2(x_2, y_2)}{MU_y^2(x_2, y_2)} = \frac{p_x}{p_y}. \tag{6.1-2}$$

Taken together, the equations of (6.1-1) and (6.1-2) geometrically describe tangencies between indifference curves and budget lines in the commodity spaces of, respectively, persons 1 and 2. Thus the final-commodity demand functions

$$x_1 = D_x^1(p_x, p_y, p_\ell, p_k),$$

$$y_1 = D_y^1(p_x, p_y, p_\ell, p_k),$$

$$x_2 = D_x^2(p_x, p_y, p_\ell, p_k),$$

$$y_2 = D_y^2(p_x, p_y, p_\ell, p_k),$$

are obtained. Because the quantities of labor and (old) capital supplied are fixed, the supply functions for these factors are constant functions:

$$\bar{\ell}_1 = S_\ell^1(p_x, p_y, p_\ell, p_k),$$

$$\bar{k}_1 = S_k^1(p_x, p_y, p_\ell, p_k),$$

$$\bar{\ell}_2 = S_\ell^2(p_x, p_y, p_\ell, p_k),$$

$$\bar{k}_2 = S_k^2(p_x, p_y, p_\ell, p_k).$$

Adding across persons gives the market demand and supply functions (table 2-1)

$$x = D_x(p_x, p_y, p_\ell, p_k),$$

$$y = D_y(p_x, p_y, p_\ell, p_k),$$

$$\bar{\ell} = S_\ell(p_x, p_y, p_\ell, p_k), \tag{6.1-3}$$

$$\bar{k} = S_k(p_x, p_y, p_\ell, p_k),$$

where $x = x_1 + x_2$, $y = y_1 + y_2$, $\bar{\ell} = \bar{\ell}_1 + \bar{\ell}_2$, and $\bar{k} = \bar{k}_1 + \bar{k}_2$.

Firms x and y have long-run production functions

$$x = F^x(\ell_x, k_x),$$
$$y = F^y(\ell_y, k_y),$$

(6.1-4)

based on existing technology. Through a cost-minimization procedure, these production functions give rise to long-run total cost functions

$$c_x = LRTC^x(x),$$
$$c_y = LRTC^y(y),$$

respectively. Firm long-run profit is expressed as

$$\pi_x = xp_x - \ell_x p_\ell - k_x p_k,$$
$$\pi_y = yp_y - \ell_y p_\ell - k_y p_k.$$

(6.1-5)

It is assumed that

$$F^x(0,0) = 0, \qquad F^y(0,0) = 0,$$

and

$$F^x(\ell_x, k_x) \geq 0, \qquad F^y(\ell_y, k_y) \geq 0,$$

for all $\ell_x \geq 0$, $k_x \geq 0$, $\ell_y \geq 0$, and $k_y \geq 0$; that both production functions are continuous with calculable marginal products (the latter are also taken to be continuous when expressed in derivative form); and that either between ridge lines or throughout the relevant input space, a larger basket of inputs gives greater output than a smaller one, and isoquants are strictly convex without touching the ℓ and k axes. Suppose also that cost curves appear as drawn in figures 4-9, 4-11, and 4-13, where marginal costs are computable (continuously, when in derivative form) and marginal cost curves slope upward beyond appropriate output levels.

Selecting inputs and outputs so as to maximize long-run profit implies that for each level of output, inputs are chosen to minimize cost. Now cost minimization means, respectively, that

$$\frac{MP_\ell^x(\ell_x)}{MP_k^x(k_x)} = \frac{p_\ell}{p_k},$$

$$\frac{MP_\ell^y(\ell_y)}{MP_k^y(k_y)} = \frac{p_\ell}{p_k},$$

$$(6.1\text{-}6)$$

while long-run profit maximization requires

$$LRMC^x(x) = p_x,$$

$$LRMC^y(y) = p_y.$$

$$(6.1\text{-}7)$$

(Equations (6.1-4) and (6.1-6) combined are the mathematical statements of tangencies between appropriate isoquants and isocost lines.) This leads, since maximum profit need not be zero in the pseudo-long-run case (sec. 5.4), to pseudo-long-run input demand functions

$$\ell_x = D_\ell^x(p_x, p_\ell, p_k),$$

$$k_x = D_k^x(p_x, p_\ell, p_k),$$

$$\ell_y = D_\ell^y(p_y, p_\ell, p_k),$$

$$k_y = D_k^y(p_y, p_\ell, p_k),$$

and pseudo-long-run output supply functions

$$x = S^x(p_x, p_\ell, p_k),$$

$$y = S^y(p_y, p_\ell, p_k),$$

for firms x and y. Because the markets for x and y each contain a single seller (firm), the latter are also the respective market supply functions in the market for x and the market for y. To be consistent with the symbolic notation of table 2-1, write them as

$$x = S_x(p_x, p_\ell, p_k),$$
$$y = S_y(p_y, p_\ell, p_k). \tag{6.1-8}$$

The market demand functions in the markets for ℓ and k are found by summing the pseudo-long-run demand functions of the individual firms:

$$\ell = D_\ell(p_x, p_y, p_\ell, p_k),$$
$$k = D_k(p_x, p_y, p_\ell, p_k), \tag{6.1-9}$$

where here $\ell = \ell_x + \ell_y$ and $k = k_x + k_y$.

With all market demand and supply functions specified, the equality of market demand and market supply is described by joining (6.1-3) to (6.1-8) and (6.1-9). Thus the market equilibrium conditions

$$D_x(p_x, p_y, p_\ell, p_k) = S_x(p_x, p_\ell, p_k),$$
$$D_y(p_x, p_y, p_\ell, p_k) = S_y(p_y, p_\ell, p_k),$$
$$D_\ell(p_x, p_y, p_\ell, p_k) = \bar{\ell}, \tag{6.1-10}$$
$$D_k(p_x, p_y, p_\ell, p_k) = \bar{k},$$

are obtained.

The Walrasian model summarized in the previous section contains sixteen major variables.

6.2 Explaining Economic Reality

> four market prices: p_x, p_y, p_ℓ, p_k,
> two market quantities: x, y,
> four individual quantities: x_1, y_1, x_2, y_2,
> four firm quantities: ℓ_x, k_x, ℓ_y, k_y,
> two profit variables: π_x, π_y,

and nine fixed parameters $\bar{\ell}_1$, $\bar{\ell}_2$, $\bar{\ell}$, $\bar{k}_1$, $\bar{k}_2$, $\bar{k}$, β_1, β_2, and α, where $\bar{\ell}_1 + \bar{\ell}_2 = \bar{\ell}$, $\bar{k}_1 + \bar{k}_2 = \bar{k}$, and $\beta_1 + \beta_2 = 1$. Any observer of the real economic world to which this model relates (described in sec. 1.1) sees only values of these variables and parameters, nothing more. Thus, for the model to explain what is seen, it is necessary that

    (i) The model determines unique values of the variables for any appropriate collection of parameter values.

   (ii) The values actually observed are accepted (interpreted) as those produced by the model.

Even though the inner workings of reality cannot be seen, as long as conditions (i) and (ii) are fulfilled, the real economy can be understood as if it had all of the characteristics of the Walrasian model. (Recall the discussions of the model of the clock in sec. 1.2 and of equilibrium in a single market in sec. 2.2.) Assent on condition (ii) is common in economics and causes no difficulties here. Condition (i), however, needs further discussion. Were it to fail, the link connecting the model with reality would be compromised.

One might think that upon specification of all parameter values, the four prices could be obtained by solving simultaneously the four demand-equals-supply equations of (6.1-10); then substitution of these prices into profit-maximization relations (6.1-7) would yield x and y; substitution of prices and the now-known x and y into (6.1-4) and (6.1-6) (the equations defining the cost-minimization tangencies) would produce ℓ_x, k_x, ℓ_y, and k_y; next, π_x and π_y would emerge from (6.1-5); and finally, x_1, y_1, x_2, and y_2 could be found by substitution into the tangency equations for utility maximization, (6.1-1) and (6.1-2). Thus it would seem that the model can be solved, thereby determining unique values for all of its variables.

There are, of course, different ways to combine equations and attempt to derive solutions. The above description is one among several possibilities. But all approaches must confront a basic problem: namely, that the four prices can only be secured by solving the four market equilibrium conditions (6.1-10), and it turns out that these conditions are not all independent of each other. Any one can always be derived from the remaining three (see app. 6.A). This means that, in general, unique solutions for all four price variables cannot exist. Moreover, since the market functions D_x, S_x, D_y, and S_y are made up of individual functions satisfying equations like (3.3-4) and (5.4-3) for all positive numbers λ, equations like (3.3-4) and (5.4-3) must also apply to D_x, S_x, D_y, and S_y. Thus the first equation, say, of (6.1-10) may be written as

$$D_x(\lambda p_x, \lambda p_y, \lambda p_\ell, \lambda p_k) = S_x(\lambda p_x, \lambda p_\ell, \lambda p_k). \qquad (6.2\text{-}1)$$

Since λ can be any positive number, one may set λ equal to the reciprocal of any of the four prices. If, for example, $\lambda = 1/p_y$, then (6.2-1) becomes

$$D_x\left(\frac{p_x}{p_y}, 1, \frac{p_\ell}{p_y}, \frac{p_k}{p_y}\right) = S_x\left(\frac{p_x}{p_y}, \frac{p_\ell}{p_y}, \frac{p_k}{p_y}\right).$$

Applying similar reasoning to the remaining equations, (6.1-10) is revealed to be actually a system of three independent equations in three price-ratio variables.[1] Hence the Walrasian model only determines unique price ratios such as

$$\frac{p_x}{p_y}, \frac{p_\ell}{p_y}, \text{ and } \frac{p_k}{p_y},$$

rather than separate unique values for each of p_x, p_y, p_ℓ, and p_k. Alternatively put, there is an infinity of different sets of four price values but only one collection of three price-ratio values that satisfy the four demand-equals-supply equations (when uniquely solvable) of the Walrasian model.

Fortunately, the fact that the Walrasian model only determines price ratios is not a serious drawback. Price ratios do indicate the rates at which one commodity exchanges for another, and this is all the information that consumers and firms require in making their utility- and profit-maximizing decisions. (For example, person 1 need only know the slope of the budget line, $-p_x/p_y$, and the term $(\alpha - z_1^0)p_\ell/p_y$ in order to arrive at the tangency in fig. 3-3(b).) Moreover, once all price ratios are

---

1. The argument reducing D_ℓ and D_k in the last two equations of (6.1-10) to functions of price ratios is trivial because the right-hand sides of these equations are constants.

found from (6.1-10), if the model is solvable, then the remaining variables may be obtained as shown earlier. Thus the important issue is not how to deal with a model that yields only price ratios, but whether or not unique solutions that involve price ratios exist at all.

It is convenient, however, to postpone discussion of these questions of existence and uniqueness until the end of this chapter, by which time the transformation curve and welfare function will have been introduced. For now, suffice it to say that there are a variety of collections of conditions, some not unlike the assumptions made here, which ensure that unique and positive values of all price ratio and other variables exist as solutions to the Walrasian model, for all appropriate parameter values. (Note that positivity of solutions rules out the zero price and zero quantity problem described in reference to market equilibrium in sect. 2.2.) Solution values of the Walrasian model are often called equilibrium values and the solution itself is referred to as an equilibrium under perfect competition, or as a competitive equilibrium, or just as an equilibrium. Equilibria, then, incorporate the notion that consumers buy final goods and sell factors so as to maximize utility subject to their budget constraints, firms hire inputs and sell outputs so as to maximize profits, demand equals supply in all markets, and all of these elements resolve themselves simultaneously. As indicated above, equilibria are also taken to be the reflection in the Walrasian model of observations of economic reality.

Before proceeding to examine further properties of Walrasian equilibrium, it is worth mentioning a few additional variables that can be defined in this Walrasian model. First of all, the incomes of persons 1 and 2 (recall equation (3.2-2)) are, respectively,

$$m_1 = \bar{\ell}_1 p_\ell + \bar{k}_1 p_k + \beta_1(\pi_x + \pi_y),$$
$$m_2 = \bar{\ell}_2 p_\ell + \bar{k}_2 p_k + \beta_2(\pi_x + \pi_y).$$

Hence to know m_1 and m_2 is to know the income distribution.

Second, "national" income in this context would be $m_1 + m_2$, and "national" expenditure $(x_1 + x_2)p_x + (y_1 + y_2)p_y$. Summing the two budget constraints of (6.1-1), then, would result in the statement that "national income equals national expenditure." Lastly, by taking consumption expenditure to be $(x_1 + x_2)p_x$, investment expenditure to be $(y_1 + y_2)p_y$, and remembering (chaps. 1 and 3) that $(y_1 + y_2)p_y$ is also aggregate savings, it follows that consumption plus savings and consumption plus investment both equal national income. Of course, the values of these variables may all be calculated at equilibrium, once equilibrium values in the Walrasian model relative to $p_y = 1$, say, are known.

Let parameters $\bar{\ell}_1$, $\bar{\ell}_2$, $\bar{\ell}$, $\bar{k}_1$, $\bar{k}_2$, $\bar{k}$, β_1, β_2, and α be given and suppose p_x^0/p_y^0, p_ℓ^0/p_y^0, p_k^0/p_y^0, x_1^0, x_2^0, x^0, y_1^0, y_2^0, y^0, ℓ_x^0, k_x^0, ℓ_y^0, k_y^0, π_x^0, and π_y^0 is the corresponding perfectly competitive equilibrium determined by the pseudo-long-run Walrasian model. Because observations of economic reality are interpreted as equilibria in the Walrasian model, any characteristics of equilibrium which can be inferred from the properties of the model automatically apply to what is seen in the real world. This section and the next are concerned with such qualities. The Pareto optimality of equilibrium is examined here while the relationship between welfare maximization and equilibrium is taken up in section 6.4.

6.3 Pareto Optimality

Think, for the moment, of the (positive) equilibrium outputs x^0 and y^0 as fixed, while the allocation of these outputs between persons 1 and 2, namely x_1, y_1, x_2, y_2, varies. Each possible distribution is pictured as a point in a consumption Edgeworth box diagram such as figure 6-1 whose size is determined by x^0 and y^0. In this diagram, person 1's coordinate system is drawn in the usual way with its origin located in the lower left-hand corner. Person 2's coordinate system, however, has been rotated so that its origin is in the upper right-hand corner. Indifference curves of person 2, then, appear (like the one labeled μ_2^*) to be upside down. Distributions such as x_1^*, y_1^*, x_2^*, y_2^*, whose components are all positive, and at which an indifference curve

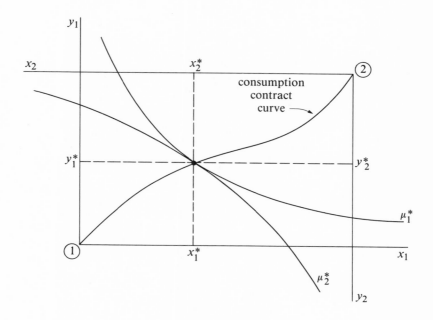

Fig. 6-1. Consumption Edgeworth box

of person 1 is tangent to an indifference curve of person 2, are optimal in consumption. (The possibility of optimal distributions on the boundary of the box, where at least one component of the distribution is zero, is not considered.) They are mathematically described (in part) by the equation

$$\frac{MU_x^1(x_1, y_1)}{MU_y^1(x_1, y_1)} = \frac{MU_x^2(x_2, y_2)}{MU_y^2(x_2, y_2)}, \qquad (6.3\text{-}1)$$

and have the property that x^0 and y^0 cannot be reallocated so as to make one person better off (i.e., to provide higher utility) without making the other worse off (with less utility). The collection of all distributions that are optimal in consumption, and only those distributions, lies on the consumption contract curve. (As defined here, the consumption contract curve in fig. 6-1 does not include its end points.)

Turning to firms x and y, regard both outputs and inputs as variable. Allocations ℓ_x, k_x, ℓ_y, k_y of the fixed amounts of

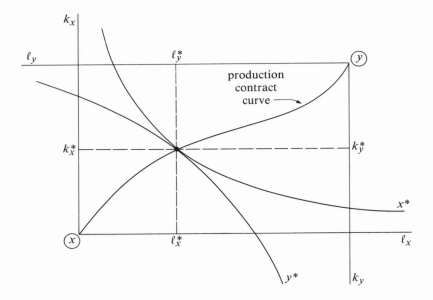

Fig. 6-2. Production Edgeworth box

labor ($\bar{\ell}$) and old capital ($\bar{k}$) between the two firms are points in a production Edgeworth box diagram, figure 6-2, which is similar to figure 6-1 except for labels. The distribution ℓ_x^*, k_x^*, ℓ_y^*, k_y^* (with all components positive) is optimal in production in that no reallocation of inputs can increase the output of one firm without lowering that of the other. The equation asserting the equality of the slopes of the appropriate isoquants at production-optimal distributions is

$$\frac{MP_\ell^x(\ell_x)}{MP_k^x(k_x)} = \frac{MP_\ell^y(\ell_y)}{MP_k^y(k_y)}. \tag{6.3-2}$$

The production contract curve is the set of all allocations that are optimal in production.

Moving from the origin of firm x to that of firm y along the production contract curve in figure 6-2, the output of firm x rises while the output of firm y falls. Plotting these outputs in figure 6-3 describes a curve called the transformation or production possibility curve. Each point on the transformation curve reflects the maximum amount of y (for example, y^* in fig. 6-3) that

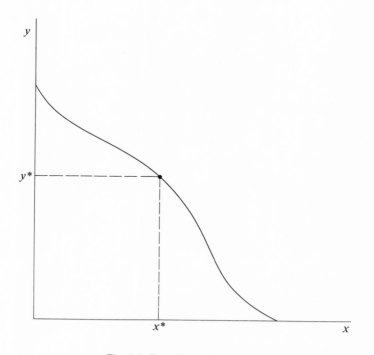

Fig. 6-3. Transformation curve

can be produced when x is fixed (at x^*). All points beneath the transformation curve are attainable but involve waste. All points beyond the transformation curve are unattainable. Thus the transformation curve shows how the economy is able to convert units of x into units of y (and vice versa), assuming that the fixed supplies of labor ($\bar{\ell}$) and old capital ($\bar{k}$) are employed as efficiently as possible in production. Indeed, the slope of the transformation curve indicates the rate (or opportunity cost) at which such conversion takes place. This slope, at the point whose coordinates on the curve are x and y, is

$$-\frac{LRMC^x(x)}{LRMC^y(y)},$$

and the same ratio without the minus sign is referred to as the marginal rate of transformation. Note that were $\bar{\ell}$ or $\bar{k}$ to change, the size of the production Edgeworth box would modify and so would the production contract curve and the transformation curve.

A distribution of final goods (outputs), x_1, y_1, x_2, y_2, between persons 1 and 2 having all components positive is called Pareto optimal if the point whose coordinates are $x_1 + x_2$ and $y_1 + y_2$ lies on the transformation curve, and if there is no other distribution of $x_1 + x_2$ and $y_1 + y_2$, and no distribution of any other output combination on the transformation curve that makes one person better off without making the other person worse off. If the distribution of final goods x_1, y_1, x_2, y_2 is Pareto optimal, then it can be shown that at appropriate points, the marginal rate of transformation is the same as each person's marginal rate of substitution, that is,

$$\frac{LRMC^x(x)}{LRMC^y(y)} = \frac{MU_x^1(x_1, y_1)}{MU_y^1(x_1, y_1)},$$
$$\frac{LRMC^x(x)}{LRMC^y(y)} = \frac{MU_x^2(x_2, y_2)}{MU_y^2(x_2, y_2)}, \qquad \text{(6.3-3)}$$

where

$$x = x_1 + x_2,$$
$$y = y_1 + y_2.$$

Since each Pareto optimal distribution is also optimal in consumption and associated with an input allocation (permitting production of the necessary outputs for distribution) that is optimal in production,[2] equations (6.3-1), (6.3-2), and (6.3-3) must hold for every Pareto optimal x_1, y_1, x_2, y_2. With some further qualifications, the converse assertion holds too: every distribution of final goods satisfying (6.3-1) and (6.3-3), such that its associated input allocation satisfies (6.3-2), is Pareto optimal.

Consider now an equilibrium such as that described at the beginning of the section: p_x^0/p_y^0, p_ℓ^0/p_y^0, p_k^0/p_y^0, x_1^0, x_2^0, x^0, y_1^0, y_2^0, y^0, ℓ_x^0, k_x^0, ℓ_y^0, k_y^0, π_x^0, and π_y^0. Substituting these values

---

2. Note, however, that a distribution that is optimal in consumption and associated with an input allocation that is optimal in production need not be Pareto optimal.

into the obvious combinations of equations (6.1-2), (6.1-6), and (6.1-7), shows that equations (6.3-1) through (6.3-3) also hold at this equilibrium. Therefore the equilibrium is Pareto optimal. Perfectly competitive equilibrium in the pseudo-long-run Walrasian model, then, has the characteristic that it wastes nothing: reallocation of inputs and outputs cannot provide greater utility to either person without taking utility away from the other.

It further turns out that for each Pareto optimal distribution (recall that, as defined, all of its components are positive), a collection of appropriate price-ratio values can be found which, when combined with the distribution, produces an equilibrium.[3] In other words, practically all Pareto optima, including those for which person 1, say, has nearly everything and person 2 has almost nothing, can arise as competitive equilibria. Therefore, in addition to nonwastefulness, equilibrium in the pseudo-long-run Walrasian model is unbiased in the sense that it can guarantee neither an equal nor a particular unequal distribution of final goods among persons. Since expenditure and income are always the same at equilibrium, this implies a similar assertion for the distribution of income: equilibrium under perfect competition is not biased in favor of any special income distribution such as equality.

6.4 Welfare Maximization

Knowing that equilibrium under perfect competition is Pareto optimal does not give any indication of whether equilibrium is the best that the economy can achieve. To see what is involved, look at the consumption Edgeworth box diagram (fig. 6-1) that emerges from some pair of outputs x and y on the transformation curve. Moving along the contract curve starting, say, from person 1's origin, the utility of person 1 increases as that of person 2 declines. Assuming

$$U^1(0,0) = 0,$$

$$U^2(0,0) = 0,$$

<hr>

3. The discussion of existence of equilibrium in the next section essentially proceeds by first locating a Pareto optimal distribution and then finding the price ratios that make it an equilibrium.

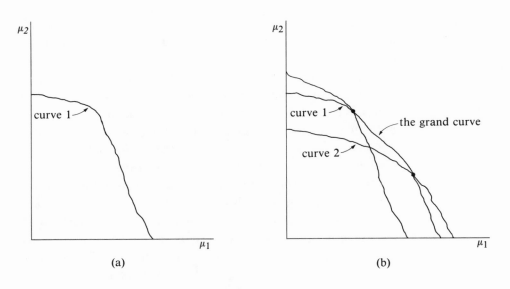

Fig. 6-4. Utility possibility curves

these utility levels may be plotted (curve 1 in fig. 6-4(a)) to yield the utility possibility curve. (A similar construction based on the production contract curve resulted in the transformation curve in sec. 6.3.) Although the utility possibility curve must slope downward, its exact shape is arbitrary because the utility numbers employed are only ordinal. Each point on the utility possibility curve corresponds to a consumption-optimal distribution on the consumption contract curve, and the curve itself is uniquely identified with the values of x and y on the transformation curve from which the Edgeworth box in which the consumption contract curve lies is secured.

Repeating the same derivation for a second point on the transformation curve gives utility possibility curve 2, which has been added to curve 1 in figure 6-4(b). Continuing for all points on the transformation curve, an entire family of utility possibility curves in the μ_1-μ_2 plane is obtained. The outer boundary of this family (also shown in fig. 6-4(b)) is the grand utility possibility curve. Each point on the grand curve lies on an ordinary utility possibility curve and, therefore, is identified with a unique point on the transformation curve, and a unique distribution on the contract curve in the associated consumption Edgeworth box. Furthermore, the distributions associated with the grand curve, and only those distributions, are Pareto optimal. (The distributions linked to points on each ordinary utility possibility curve are, in general, only optimal in consumption.)

Of course, it seems impossible to tell which of any two points on the same utility possibility curve is better than the other, because in moving between them, the utility of one person goes up while that of the other drops. For the same reason, a similar comparison of two points on the grand curve seems incapable of being made. (It could be said, however, that a point on one ordinary curve is better than a point on another if the utility of both persons is greater at the former point. Thus, according to this criterion, points on the grand curve are usually better then at least some points on every ordinary curve.) Even so, all noncomparabilities can be eliminated by introducing a welfare function.

Insert a new entity into the pseudo-long-run Walrasian model called "society." Like the individual described in section 3.1, let society have preferences and indifferences among baskets of utilities (μ_1, μ_2), and suppose that these preferences and indifferences are represented by a welfare function

$$\omega = W(\mu_1, \mu_2),$$

that assigns higher levels of "welfare," ω, to more preferred baskets. Assume also that W has the same properties attributed to individual utility functions in section 3.1. Clearly, such a welfare function cannot be defined without making value judgments concerning the relative "importance" of each individual in the determination of society's preferences.

However, once such a welfare function has been specified, no matter how arbitrarily, the best basket of utilities available to society can be found by maximizing W subject to the grand utility possibility curve. In the illustration of figure 6-5, the best basket is (μ_1', μ_2'), where the ω' welfare-indifference curve is tangent to the grand curve. As indicated above, (μ_1', μ_2') is associated with some Pareto optimal distribution of final goods.

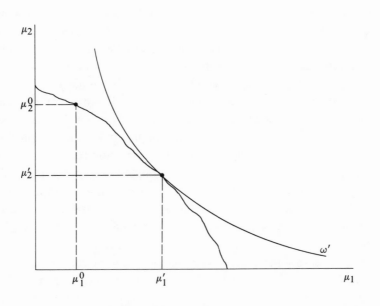

Fig. 6-5. Welfare maximization subject to the grand utility possibility curve

Thus equilibrium under perfect competition is Pareto optimal and at least one Pareto optimal distribution is identified with welfare maximization. But just as a particular distribution of income cannot be ensured, so it does not follow that equilibrium under perfect competition always maximizes society's welfare. Whether equilibrium maximizes welfare or not depends on what the welfare function is. And there is no reason why perfectly competitive equilibrium cannot leave the economy at, say, (μ_1^0, μ_2^0) in figure 6-5, somewhere short of maximum welfare. Regardless, these conclusions provide the basis, under perfectly competitive conditions, for Adam Smith's assertion that an "invisible hand" leads individuals motivated by self-interest to promote an end (Pareto optimality and possibly even welfare maximization) that they do not intend and that is in the interest of society at large.[4]

---

4. A. Smith, *An Inquiry into the Nature and Causes of the Wealth of Nations* (New York: Random House, 1937), 423.

**6.5
Existence and
Uniqueness
of Equilibria**

It has already been pointed out that in the Walrasian model a great deal turns on whether equilibrium exists and is unique. If unique equilibrium did not exist in the model, then observations of the real world could not be identified with such equilibria, and thus no explanation of reality based on unique equilibrium, including the Walrasian explanation erected above, could be given. Obviously, too, analyses relating equilibrium to Pareto optima and welfare maximization would become vacuous and irrelevant.

In general, to properly consider questions of existence and uniqueness requires mathematics well beyond the level and scope of present discussion. The flavor of the problem can still be transmitted, however, by introducing several additional assumptions that further simplify the (already highly simplified) model of this chapter.

Referring to equations (6.1-1), say, assume first that the quantities of labor ($\bar{\ell}_1$ and $\bar{\ell}_2$) and old capital ($\bar{k}_1$ and $\bar{k}_2$) supplied by the two persons, along with the fractions of combined profit distributed to each (β_1 and β_2), are the same. That is,

$$\bar{\ell}_1 = \bar{\ell}_2,$$

$$\bar{k}_1 = \bar{k}_2,$$

and, since it has previously been required that $\beta_1 + \beta_2 = 1$,

$$\beta_1 = \beta_2 = \frac{1}{2}.$$

The next assumption is that persons 1 and 2 have identical utility functions or, in other words, that

$$U^1(x_1, y_1) = U^2(x_2, y_2),$$

whenever $x_1 = x_2$ and $y_1 = y_2$. (Recall that leisure time z has been dropped as an argument of these functions because it is fixed.) Taken together, these assumptions mean that, insofar as the present Walrasian model is concerned, there is no difference between the two individuals.

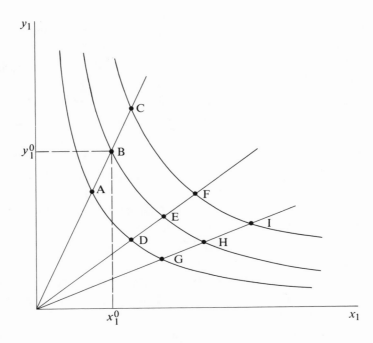

Fig. 6-6. Homothetic indifference map

The last assumption to be made imposes a very special property on individual utility functions: varying the quantities of any basket of commodities in the same proportion has no effect on the marginal rate of substitution or the slope of the indifference curve at that basket. Thus, for example, the slopes of the three indifference curves of person 1 in figure 6-6 are the same at points A, B, and C (where the basket at A is derived by multiplying both of the components of (x_1^0, y_1^0) by the same positive number less than 1, and that at C is derived by multiplying both x_1^0 and y_1^0 by the same number larger than 1). Similarly the three indifference curves have identical slopes at D, E, and F, and at G, H, and I. (Of course, the slope of, say, the lowest indifference curve varies from A to D to G.) Indifference maps exhibiting this property are called homothetic.

Now, under the above additional assumptions, it is possible

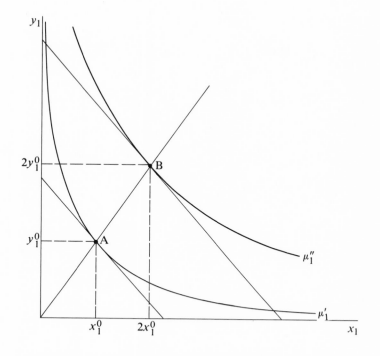

Fig. 6-7. Derivation of the community utility function

to construct a utility function for the "community" as a whole (consisting, in this case, of persons 1 and 2) which, when maximized subject to an aggregate budget constraint, yields the market demand functions for x and y. In terms of indifference maps, the construction can be exhibited as follows. With all parameters specified and all market prices given, utility maximization subject to the budget constraint for person 1 can be pictured in two dimensions at, say, the point A in figure 6-7. Since person 2 is identical to person 1, person 2's utility-maximizing position may also be thought of as at point A with the same indifference curve μ_1', the same budget line, and the same basket (x_1^0, y_1^0). Thus, at the given prices, market quantities demanded (which are the sum of individual quantities demanded) are $2x_1^0$ and $2y_1^0$, and this basket of market demands is located at point B. By the homotheticity of person 1's indifference map, there is an indifference curve μ_1'' through

B having the same slope at B that μ_1' has at A. Furthermore, the aggregate budget line can be secured by graphing the sum of the individual constraint equations in (6.1-1), that is, by graphing

$$xp_x + yp_y = \bar{\ell}p_\ell + \bar{k}p_k + \pi_x + \pi_y, \qquad (6.5\text{-}1)$$

where $x = x_1 + x_2$, $y = y_1 + y_2$, $\bar{\ell} = \bar{\ell}_1 + \bar{\ell}_2$, $\bar{k} = \bar{k}_1 + \bar{k}_2$, and where π_x and π_y are, respectively, the (maximum) profits obtained by firms x and y given all parameters and prices. This aggregate budget line passes through B and has the same slope as the budget line through A. Therefore market demand quantities at the given configuration of prices can be derived by maximizing U^1 (or, equivalently, U^2) subject to the aggregate budget constraint (6.5-1), and then the quantities demanded by the individuals at the same prices can be calculated by dividing the market quantities so obtained in half. When person 1's utility function is used in this way it is referred to as a community utility function. Community utility functions are generally not welfare functions. There is no reason for the preferences and indifferences of the community as a whole (society) to be the same as those that underlie the derivation of market demand functions from a community utility function.

Superimposing the indifference map from the community utility function constructed above on the transformation-curve diagram of figure 6-3, it is clear that community utility is maximized at a tangency between one of the indifference curves and the transformation curve—for example, at A in figure 6-8. Let p_x^0/p_y^0 be the negative of the slope of the straight line simultaneously tangent to this indifference curve and the transformation curve at A. Since the market quantities at A, namely x^0 and y^0, lie on an indifference curve from the community utility function, they correspond to a distribution of outputs among the two individuals of

$$x_1^0 = x_2^0 = \frac{1}{2}x^0,$$

$$y_1^0 = y_2^0 = \frac{1}{2}y^0.$$

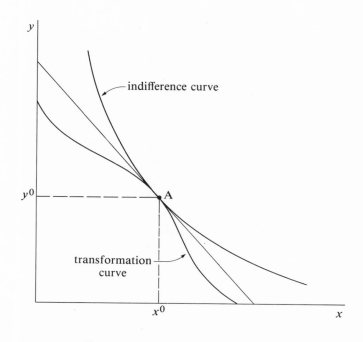

Fig. 6-8. Existence of unique equilibrium

And since these same market quantities also lie on the transformation curve, they are further associated (recall the derivation of fig. 6-3 from fig. 6-2) with a distribution of inputs among the two firms that lies on the production contract curve in the appropriate production Edgeworth box. Denote this second distribution by $\ell_x^0, k_x^0, \ell_y^0, k_y^0$, where $\ell_x^0 + \ell_y^0 = \bar{\ell}$ and $k_x^0 + k_y^0 = \bar{k}$. Lastly, set the ratios p_ℓ^0/p_y^0 and p_k^0/p_y^0, respectively, according to the equations

$$\frac{p_\ell^0}{p_y^0} = MP_\ell^y(\ell_y^0, k_y^0),$$

$$(6.5\text{-}2)$$

$$\frac{p_k^0}{p_y^0} = MP_k^y(\ell_y^0, k_y^0).$$

(These equations are the analogues for firm y to those for firm x in (5.4-2). It is not necessary to add (5.4-2) to (6.5-2) because the equations for firm x are already implied. See app. 6.B.) Then the three required price ratios p_x/p_y, p_ℓ/p_y, and p_k/p_y, and all individual and market quantities are determined. Since the indifference and transformation curves in figure 6-8 are drawn smoothly without kinks at A, and since they also have a nonlinear curvature at A, the output price ratio and all output and output-distribution quantities are unique. Uniqueness of the input quantities follows from the construction of the transformation curve, and uniqueness of the remaining price ratios (6.5-2) obtains from the single-valuedness of the marginal product functions. Moreover, at these price ratios and quantities, both individuals are maximizing utility subject to their budget constraints, both firms are maximizing profit, and supply equals demand in all four markets. Therefore, equilibrium in this simplified Walrasian model exists and is unique.

Appendix 6.A   The proposition that not all equations of (6.1-10) are independent of each other follows from an equation known as Walras' law. In the present context it is proved as follows. Add the two equations of (6.1-1) and use the fact $\beta_1 + \beta_2 = 1$ so that

$$(x_1 + x_2)p_x + (y_1 + y_2)p_y = \bar{\ell}p_\ell + \bar{k}p_k + \pi_x + \pi_y,$$

where $\bar{\ell} = \bar{\ell}_1 + \bar{\ell}_2$ and $\bar{k} = \bar{k}_1 + \bar{k}_2$. Now sum the two equations of (6.1-5) to obtain

$$\pi_x + \pi_y = xp_x + yp_y - (\ell_x + \ell_y)p_\ell - (k_x + k_y)p_k.$$

Next use the second equation to substitute for $\pi_x + \pi_y$ in the first, use (6.1-8) to eliminate x and y, use (6.1-9) to eliminate $\ell_x + \ell_y$ and $k_x + k_y$, and use (6.1-3) to eliminate $(x_1 + x_2)$ and $(y_1 + y_2)$. The result is Walras' law:

$$
\begin{aligned}
0 = {}& p_x \left[D_y(p_x, p_y, p_\ell, p_k) - S_x(p_x, p_\ell, p_k) \right] \\
&+ p_y \left[D_y(p_x, p_y, p_\ell, p_k) - S_y(p_y, p_\ell, p_k) \right] \\
&+ p_\ell \left[D_\ell(p_x, p_y, p_\ell, p_k) - \bar{\ell} \right] \\
&+ p_k \left[D_k(p_x, p_y, p_\ell, p_k) - \bar{k} \right].
\end{aligned}
$$

Clearly, any three market equilibrium conditions imply the fourth.

The assertion that, at equilibrium, the equations of (5.4-2) are   **Appendix 6.B**
implied in the construction of section 6.5 is demonstrated as
follows. Using, in order, the first equation of (6.5-2), the equation
reflecting the equality of slopes of the transformation curve and
tangent line in figure 6-8, namely

$$\frac{LRMC^x(x^0)}{LRMC^y(y^0)} = \frac{p_x^0}{p_y^0},$$

and the fact (not discussed here) that

$$\frac{LRMC^x(x^0)}{LRMC^y(y^0)} = \frac{MP_\ell^y(\ell_y^0, k_y^0)}{MP_\ell^x(\ell_x^0, k_x^0)},$$

gives

$$\frac{p_\ell^0}{p_x^0} = \frac{p_y^0}{p_x^0}\frac{p_\ell^0}{p_y^0} = \frac{p_y^0}{p_x^0}MP_\ell^y(\ell_y^0, k_y^0),$$

$$= \frac{LRMC^y(y^0)}{LRMC^x(x^0)}MP_\ell^y(\ell_y^0, k_y^0),$$

$$= \frac{MP_\ell^x(\ell_x^0, k_x^0)}{MP_\ell^y(\ell_y^0, k_y^0)}MP_\ell^y(\ell_y^0, k_y^0),$$

$$= MP_\ell^x(\ell_x^0, k_x^0).$$

This is the first equation of (5.4-2). A similar argument applies
for the second.

7   The Walrasian Vision

The Walrasian vision is a mental image of the economic world and the way it operates. Previous chapters have attempted to articulate this vision by setting out a particular Walrasian model and, in the process, many of the forms interwoven in the Walrasian image have appeared. But the model is not unique. There are numerous Walrasian-type models that spring from and are consistent with the Walrasian vision. Although such models differ in detail, all share certain similarities by virtue of their common source. These shared features, which define the Walrasian vision to a considerable extent, are now summarized briefly.

The Walrasian image contains consumers and firms. Consumers make decisions about purchases of final commodities and sales of the resources (factors) they possess. Firms make determinations concerning how much output to produce and with what inputs. Output determinations are selling decisions; input determinations are buying decisions. All consumer and firm decisions interact simultaneously through markets, and the resolution of these interactions results in equilibrium, that is, a state of rest over time or steady state. (In the present volume, equilibrium, and only equilibrium, is interpreted to be that which is seen in reality. Such an interpretation, though typical, is not necessary to the Walrasian vision and is easily and often dropped.)

The institutional structure of markets is perfectly competitive. Thus within any one market there are "large" numbers

of "small" buyers and sellers, the market's commodity is standardized, entry into the market is free, and the same perfect
information is available to all of the market's participants. In
part, these traits imply that firms and consumers perceive prices
as elements over which they have no control.

Consumer decisions are based on preferences expressed in
utility functions. Given market prices, the baskets of final
commodities and factors they want to buy and sell are selected
by maximizing utility subject to budget constraints. Utility
functions possess sufficient properties so that such constrained
maximization can be carried out. As consumers face alternative
hypothetical price configurations, repeated maximization generates consumption demand and factor supply functions. All
properties assumed of utility functions are reflected as restrictions
imposed on these latter derived functions.

Firms, on the other hand, are confronted by technology in
the form of production functions. Subject also to given market
prices, they hire inputs and produce outputs so as to maximize
profits. Individual input demand and output supply functions
are secured as the prices of inputs and output vary (in theory)
and the maximization is repeated. Once again it is necessary
to require production functions to exhibit properties sufficient to
ensure that profit maximization can be accomplished, and these
properties force input demand and output supply functions to
take on corresponding characteristics.

Combining the relevant demand and supply functions of
all participants in any market gives, respectively, the market's
demand and supply functions. Markets operate by balancing
off the forces of demand and supply within them: market
equilibrium arises when market demand equals market supply.

Markets, of course, do not operate in isolation. Changes
in one bring about changes in others. Indeed, in an economy
with, say, N markets ($N = 4$ in the model of chaps. 2 through
6), if any $N - 1$ of them are in equilibrium together, then so
is the Nth. In general, equilibrium occurs when all consumers
are buying final outputs and selling factors so as to maximize
utility subject to budget constraints, all firms are hiring inputs
and producing outputs which maximize profits, and supply equals
demand in all markets. Such an equilibrium is Pareto optimal

in that outputs can be neither feasibly enlarged nor redistributed among consumers so as to increase the utility of one person without lowering that of someone else, and the output of any firm cannot be expanded except by reducing production in another. Moreover, the distribution of outputs associated with equilibrium may or may not equalize across individuals, and may or may not maximize social welfare, depending on the nature of society's welfare function.

There are, finally, certain aspects of the Walrasian vision that have not been explicitly formalized in the presentation of the Walrasian model of chapters 2 through 6. The most important of these is, perhaps, the way in which the vision incorporates change.[1] After all, focusing attention on the steady state, as chapters 2 through 6 do, obviously precludes any serious discussion of change. For processes of change can only manifest themselves out of equilibrium as, for example, in moving from one equilibrium to another. (Thus the identification here of sightings of reality with equilibria renders impossible the observation of such processes at work. To be able to see change unfold, then, necessitates the discarding of this interpretation. But even when the interpretation is maintained, processes of change can still be conceived of hypothetically, if not actually observed.) While the explication of change in Walrasian models is beyond the limits of present discussion, the Walrasian vision of at least one well-known process of change is easily described.

Starting out of equilibrium, as the activities of producing, buying, and selling cause goods to flow through markets in exchange for payments (fig. 1-1), shortages and surpluses arise. The markets respond by sending signals to producers: in the case of shortages, prices and hence profits are relatively high; for surpluses they are relatively low. Producers, in turn, react to these price signals by making decisions that have the impact of diverting resources from the production of goods with low profits to the production of those with high profits. The process continues until, upon achieving equilibrium, all shortages and surpluses disappear.

---

1. The idea of change (or movement) has been hinted at, for example, in the discussions of equilibrium and stability in section 2.2 and of free entry in the long run in section 5.4. It was also mentioned in the description of the economy in section 1.1.

Dynamic processes such as these, which operate within and among the markets of the economy, give form to Adam Smith's notion of an invisible hand that guides maximizing individuals and firms who pursue their own self-interest. Thus, provided these processes converge to equilibrium, as they usually are assumed to do in the Walrasian vision, it can be said that the invisible hand leads the economy toward an end which is at least Pareto optimal, if not always welfare-maximizing.

The importance of the Walrasian vision lies in the intellectual and social usefulness of the analyses that spring from it. But there is much more than that. For the Walrasian vision has a power all its own that has transcended its usefulness and allowed it to become the basis for a substantial portion of modern economic thought. This power stems not only from the success of the investigations it has inspired, but also, in part, from its suggestion that even though the Walrasian vision is an abstraction, a crude approximation of economic reality, there would still appear to be coherence in economic life. Furthermore, the outcomes of such coherence can be evaluated and ethical judgments made about them. In the context of a Walrasian model, these outcomes are the equilibria, the solutions, that depend on parameter values. Although the model itself permits efficiency judgments about its outcomes in the analysis of their Pareto optimality, ethical evaluations of them are left for expression in terms of a general but unspecified welfare function. Thus the options open to society through the selection of parameter values are set out with considerable clarity and precision. It is this image of a well-defined collection of outcomes among which society may choose, each consistent with the self-interest-motivated or maximizing behavior that reflects the strong current of individualism present in Western thought and culture, that makes the Walrasian vision so popular and so appealing.

The Walrasian vision is, of course, only one of many contributions that the discipline of economics can make to the understanding of economic society and the achievement of economic objectives. Alternative visions exist and still others may emerge as time passes. Indeed, given the endless creative energy of the human mind, the potential is unlimited. All the same, the Walrasian vision stands as an imposing achievement in its own right, and, moreover, in the hands of skilled and judicious practitioners, as a potentially significant advance on the road toward social improvement.

Index